TRAILBLAZER

A WOMAN'S GUIDE TO LETTING GO OF
EXPECTATIONS, TRUSTING YOURSELF, AND
CREATING THE PATH TO A FULFILLING LIFE

CHAUNDELL MONN

DEDICATION

"She was wild and untamed
She was a wanderer
No matter how she tried
There were times when she just had to
Run
But rather
Than try to change her
Trap her
Tame her
He simply ran
Beside her"

—Louise Alexandra Erskine

This book is dedicated to my husband, Will, who always sees my potential, loves me for who I am, and never tries to tame me. Your strength, patience, and love inspire me every day. Life would be 99.9 percent less fun without you.

DOWNLOAD YOUR FREE WORKBOOK

Throughout this book there are self-reflection and action steps to help guide you on your journey. This workbook takes all the prompts throughout the book and puts them in one place for you to write your insights and reflections.

To download, go to

www.chaundellmonn.com/trailblazerworkbook

"I will not follow where the path may lead, but I will go where there is no path, and I will leave a trail."

—MURIEL STRODE

TABLE OF CONTENTS

SECTION 4: CLEAR YOUR PATH

SECTION 5: LIVING A DARING LIFE

PROLOGUE

What do I want my life to look like in five years?"

I sat cross-legged on the floor in the church. The chairs were all stacked up and pushed against the walls so the floors could be vacuumed on Saturday. In the quiet, almost still room, I looked around at the other girls who were thinking and writing while I sat there staring at a blank piece of paper and a pencil that refused to move. I knew I had a time limit, so I felt rushed, and my brain panicked. What if I still had a blank page when the time was up? I was supposed to write down what I wanted my life to look like in five years and seal it in an envelope. In five years, I would be twenty-three years old. My church leader would send our letters to us so we could see what our past selves wrote, and see if our life turned out how we wanted it to. It sounded like a cute idea at the time.

Each second seemed to pass quickly, yet to me, time seemed to move as slow as mud. I realized the reason I didn't have any words on my paper was not that I didn't know what to write. I did know. I was just too afraid to write my goals down because I didn't know if it was "right" to want them.

Growing up in a conservative religion, church leaders and my family taught me that I should want to be a stay-at-home mother and take care of my kids. They said that was the greatest thing I could do with my life, that it was my main purpose. However, I really wanted to go to school and get an education. I wanted to work and have a successful career. I wanted to travel to places like Italy and France because I had a newfound love for art history, and I wanted to see all the artwork I learned about with my own eyes. While I did want to be married at some point, it was an idea for the far future—although, for the right guy, I could be flexible with that timeline. But I also didn't have a desire to have children. Well, actually, deep down, I really did want children, but being the oldest of seven kids, I felt like I had already helped raise a few kids. So I was ready to do what I wanted to do for once, and I guess I didn't think I could have that while also having kids.

I had to make a decision: would I write down the life I was taught I should want, or would I write the true desires of my heart?

I started writing, and with each word that I wrote, I became more confident. As I wrote out the true desires of my heart that day, I decided that I was going to own it, and I looked hopefully toward my future life.

Five Years Later

I forgot all about that letter not too long after I'd written it. I'm not sure I ever really expected it to make its way to me. After all, five years is a long time to hold on to something without losing it. So, I was surprised when I got a phone call from my parents and siblings. They were gathered together, and, on speakerphone, told me they received a letter for me from an unknown sender. By then, I had moved out of the house and was living in a different state. I had forgotten that this letter existed and didn't remember what it said, so I just had them open it up and read it to me over the phone—which I quickly regretted.

They read all my teenage hopes and dreams out loud so everyone could hear. My family kept erupting in peals of laughter. I was laughing, too, but truthfully, I was also really embarrassed. For one, remember how I said that I'd consider an earlier timeline for marriage for the right guy? Apparently, I had an idea of who that could've been because I mentioned Aaron, the boy I had a crush on in high school, by name.

Ugh. So embarrassing.

Second, guess how many of the things I listed in that letter had actually come true?

—NONE of them.—

There I was, five years later—a married, stay-at-home-mom with twins, never having traveled anywhere outside the United States, no degree to my name, and no career.

There is absolutely nothing wrong with any of those things, but I felt conflicted inside. Without a doubt, I loved my husband and my children, and I wouldn't want to go back and give them up, but I also meant what I wrote back then, too.

I fake-laughed it off to my family, and brushed off the letter as silly teen stuff, but I felt really sad. Like, really sad. It wasn't just because I didn't get to live my dreams; it was more than that. I felt like I had sold out in some way. Like I'd betrayed the courageous version of me that had written the truth in my heart. It seemed like such a waste to feel so empowered, so determined, and so *honest* just to do nothing with it.

INTRODUCTION

"Why am I so unhappy?"

I know for a fact that I'm not the only woman in this world who's asked herself this. I've seen and met women at church, at my children's school, on Facebook, on Instagram, and at many girls' nights out who aren't happy in their lives. They are unfulfilled and feel their lives lack purpose as they complete daily tasks just to survive each day, yet they feel like it all means nothing. I've listened to many moms who love their kids but resent all the sacrifices they have made. I've talked to women who don't have children, or women whose children are grown up and now they're struggling to know their purpose. Women who hate that they have to work, and women who wish they could have a career. Women who have a lot of hobbies they don't have time for. And women who don't even know who they are or what they like anymore. You get it. There are a lot of unhappy women out there. To top off this unhappiness sundae, they all feel guilty about being unhappy. 'Cause here's the kicker: these women who say they're unhappy also feel very grateful for their lives. Now, that's something that resonates with me.

Five years after I received that letter in the mail, I was in a dark place. Even though I would often think my life had turned out pretty well, I would wonder why I was so unhappy.

This thought always came with guilt.

The truth was that I really did have a great life, and it really was better than I thought possible. My husband had a well-paying job, and we lived in a brand-new house in a safe, quiet neighborhood. We had three boys, and I got to stay home and raise them.

From the outside, no one would be able to see anything was wrong. I was high-functioning, as they say, accomplishing everything that needed to be done. I went through the motions: cleaning, grocery shopping, cooking, playing with the kids, and volunteering at church and the boys' school. What I decided to do, I made sure I did well.

On the inside, though, I was suffering. The monotony of everyday life was weighing me down. I felt unhappy and unfulfilled. This nagging feeling within called for something more. It was like something was missing in my life. I kept this feeling to myself because I was ashamed. I felt ungrateful and maybe a little bit afraid that, ultimately, the problem was me, not my life. That's a pretty common fear for me.

From as far back as I can remember, I've never really fit in anywhere. I learned how to fit in enough, but no matter where I went, there was always a part of me that didn't fit into whatever box I attempted to put myself in. I told myself that meant that I wasn't trying hard enough or that I just wasn't enough.

Within the next couple of years, in an attempt to fit into this life I had created, I grasped for anything that would satisfy the nagging feeling. I tried to do some self-care by starting a couple of side businesses from home, joining a gym and working out regularly, and taking steps to be more organized and better with time management. When those tactics only worked temporarily, I tried to drown out the nagging by scrolling social media, binge-watching shows on my DVR, and engaging in emotional eating. Those only worked temporarily, too; the feeling always returned. I had no idea what to do, so I just kept trying to ignore it. But the Universe had different plans for me and decided to intervene with a mystery sickness. The mystery sickness led to going to therapy, which led me to psychology and the self-help world. Previously, I had always looked down on the self-help world with all its pep talks and meditation-y woo-woo stuff. It was too out there for me, and I turned my nose up at it. But at my low point, I was desperate, and the woo-woo was the only thing I hadn't tried—and it ended up being the thing that saved me. Not only saved me, totally transformed me. It helped me take all my broken pieces and turn them into a beautiful mosaic of awesomeness. It was the missing piece I didn't know was missing, and when I found it, my life started changing drastically.

Why I Wrote This Book

It took me years to figure out why I was so unhappy. Years! And, to be honest, if the Universe hadn't kicked me in the butt, it would've probably taken me even longer. The reason I didn't start sooner was I didn't know what to do, and I didn't know how to do it. I didn't even know what I was trying to do, other than go from unhappy to happy. That's pretty vague and left no clue of where to start. Being a book nerd, I started with what I did best, which was reading a lot of books. Two books that stood out to me were *Eat, Pray, Love* by Elizabeth Gilbert and *Wild* by Cheryl Strayed. I loved them and didn't love them, all at the same time. I loved that they both had this journey of self-discovery. I loved that both authors freed themselves from expectations and started over, intentionally creating a more fulfilling life. What I didn't love is how they did it. I love the outdoors, but I'm zero percent interested in backpacking anywhere. Solo travel sounded fun but unrealistic for me, with three young kids to take care of. Also, they both decided to get divorced, which was not something I was interested in at all. They both left their old life completely behind to start over, and I didn't want to do that. It left me wondering if I could get the same results, but do it differently. That gave birth to this book, my process, and my life.

The Real Problem

The reason so many of us are living unfulfilling lives really boils down to one thing: the inner battle. I've always felt this inner tug of war in my heart. It's kind of like a devil and angel on your shoulder situation, except I wasn't sure if the contradictions represented good versus bad. The thoughts from both sides seemed like they came from me, yet they were telling me different things. I was so confused. How could they both be me?

What I've learned is that we are spiritual beings having a human experience. We existed before in a nonphysical state. In that state, we were learning, and we brought all of that knowledge with us to Earth, where the nonphysical part of us joined with our body, the physical part of us. We don't consciously remember our nonphysical state, but those memories are in our subconscious. And death is not the end for us. We'll continue to exist when we leave our physical form, and whatever we learn here, we'll take with us. Our spirit, energy, whatever you want to call it, is one of the angels/devils. In this book, we'll call this dynamic the Inner Compass. But, there is another part. When we get our physical bodies, we gain an addition to our consciousness. We'll call this part the Natural Instinct. These two parts both make up our consciousness, but they are very different. The thoughts that come from each of these parts say different things, which means that your reality, your life, will turn out differently, depending on which voice you listen to.

The Natural Instinct is all about survival. Its main focus and purpose are to keep us alive. It believes death is the end, so the fear of death is a strong motivator. Since being rejected or kicked out of a group literally meant death for our ancestors, we now have a strong desire to fit in and belong to a group. Thus, when we are living by our Natural Instinct, we fall into comparison, fear, people-pleasing, and focusing on the past and everything outside of ourselves.

Our Inner Compass is the part of us that existed before we were in our physical bodies. It looks into the future and is not focused on daily survival, but long-term growth. It's focused on guiding you to fulfill your potential. It's the oldest, wisest, deepest part of who you are. When we're living by our Inner Compass, we're acting from love, looking for opportunities for growth, and focusing on who we want to be. The focus is internal rather than external.

Our most fulfilling lives happen when we follow our Inner Compass, but most of us are following our Natural Instinct because that is what we're taught to do as children. At times, our Natural Instinct and Inner Compass influence us to want the same thing, so they can work harmoniously, but other times, they're at odds with each other, and you have to choose which one you'll follow. The biggest problem is we aren't taught the difference between the two, and because of this, we tend to favor our Natural Instincts over our Inner Compass. If we want to live authentic, purposeful, fulfilling, and happy lives, we need to learn how to live from our Inner Compass.

In the end, this is what Elizabeth Gilbert and Cheryl Strayed learned how to do. They dropped the expectations that come from living based on Natural Instinct, and they learned how to tune into their Inner Compass. By connecting to that part of themselves, they were able to change the course of their lives and start intentionally creating the lives that they wanted. It is a journey that every author in any self-discovery book I've read has had to make. While each author wanted different things and their journeys looked different, they all had one thing in common: they're all Trailblazers.

It's Your Time

I'm going to go out on a limb and assume that this may be the first time someone has told you that it's OK to blaze your own trail. I'm not only going to tell you it's OK, but that it is necessary if you want to live a fulfilling, purposeful, and authentic life. As children, we have been conditioned to believe that we need permission from others to do what we want to do or be who we want to be. At school, you have to raise your hand and ask to speak or ask to go to the bathroom. In the home, you have to ask for a snack, whether you can hang out with your friends, or if you can be excused from the dinner table. This belief of needing to ask for permission doesn't just go away, as an adult. You may feel like you have to get permission from your spouse to spend money on yourself. You feel like you need to ask for permission to go after your dreams, or worse, to even dream at all. Asking for permission is one of those "rules" that we've just been accepting as truth, when, in reality, it's a rule that you get to decide whether to follow or not. It doesn't mean that you don't have a discussion with your spouse about your dreams or spending money, but there is a difference between expressing your needs and discussing how you can make them happen and asking whether it's OK for you to want or do those things. You really don't need anyone's permission to live a life you love, and you definitely don't need anyone's permission to do it in your own way, but if you've been waiting for someone to say it to you, today is the day. I want you to go find a mirror and stand in front of it. Look the woman staring back at you in the eyes and say, "I give you permission to be you."

You're at a fork in the road. You can close this book and continue living your life exactly how you're living it right now, but if you do, what will your life look like in one year? Five years? Ten years? I can tell you from experience that if you keep doing and thinking the same things, you'll keep creating the same results. Would you be OK if your life stayed the same for the next ten years? If not, then it's time for a change. It's time for a new path.

This book is for you if:

- You've been wanting to change your life, but you don't know how.

- Your life is overwhelmed with to-do lists, obligations, and boring tasks, and you suspect there's more for you.

- You know you have a bigger purpose than you're currently living, but you don't know how to identify it.

- You want more time to do the things you love with the people you love the most.

This book is not for you if:

- You're not open to challenging your thoughts, beliefs, or actions.

- You don't believe in some kind of higher power (God, Universe, Source Energy, etc.).

- You're not willing to take action.

So many people on this Earth live each day searching for the one thing that will help them live their best life, but the answer isn't out there. The secret sauce to living your best life is already within you. You just need to listen to it and act. Your daring life is waiting for you, and it begins with the first step. Turn the page and I'll meet you on the trail.

SECTION 1

WHAT IS A TRAILBLAZER?

CHAPTER ONE

TO BE A TRAILBLAZER

To be a Trailblazer means to make a new path, rather than following already established paths. When you decide to surrender to your Inner Compass, you're choosing to step off the path you've been put on and make a different one. A Trailblazer looks at her life in a different way than other people. She challenges her past way of thinking, makes her own rules, trusts herself, and intentionally chooses actions that help her get what she wants and be who she wants to be.

A Daring Life

The results of trailblazing are self-discovery and a life that's more beautiful and amazing than you could have imagined. It's more beautiful because it has less of what you *should* be and more of what you *want* to be. The journey to get there will look different for all of us. Cheryl Strayed's journey looked like ninety-four days on the Pacific Crest Trail. Elizabeth Gilbert's looked like leaving it all and traveling to Italy, India, and Bali for a year. My journey took five years and looked like adopting, traveling with my family, taking an unconventional job, and moving to the Pacific Northwest, along with a lot of other small changes. None of us did it the wrong way. We did it *our* way, and we all got the same result in the end. We got what I call a daring life.

A daring life is doing what you know is right for you, regardless of what others think. It is seeing yourself as an individual and a person worthy of development. It's a life that is aligned with the values and beliefs you've chosen for yourself. Because it takes courage to change and try something new, you have to dare to achieve it. It's daring to stand out and be different, and possibly not be liked by someone. It's daring to trust yourself over the many voices outside of you, to live a life on your terms.

Below are just some of the changes and benefits that can show up from being a Trailblazer and living a daring life:

- You have more time to spend on the things that really matter to you.

- You can be more present and available to those you love.

- The opinions of others no longer affect your sense of value or your choices.

- You have time to do the things that you love.

- You wake up each day excited to live your life.

- You go to bed each night knowing that what you do matters and has a purpose.

- You love yourself and no longer need to seek out love and validation from others.

- You're dreaming bigger, because you believe your dreams are possible.

- You can fully be yourself without fear of rejection.

Building a daring life and being a Trailblazer go hand in hand. You must be willing to step off the path cleared by other people and start creating a new path that is uniquely yours.

Your Life. Your Rules.

To create this daring life, you need to set the rules. Once, a friend texted me a picture of an outfit with two pairs of shoes. She wanted to know which pair I thought looked best with the outfit. I picked the one I liked, but she was hesitant because she didn't know what else she could wear them with. I gave her color options, one of them being white. She said she had a white skirt that she could wear them with, but she didn't think she could wear white after Labor Day because of the fashion "rules." I texted back, "I don't follow fashion rules. I make my own rules."

I'm kind of a we're-not-gonna-take-it/no-one-puts-baby-in-a-corner type of girl.

I'm all about the girl power.

I wasn't always this way, though. As a little girl, I wasn't taught to allow myself this kind of power. We're taught to be self-sacrificing and accommodating. To not be too loud or too big. We're given badges of honor when we put everyone else before ourselves, because that's what "good girls" do. We're taught that it's selfish for us to think of our wants and needs. These rules often kept me small and limited to what I thought I could become. As an adult, I've found that the rules haven't changed much. To be a "good mom," you should be self-sacrificing and accommodating. Women who are too loud or whose personalities are too big are considered obnoxious (or worse). If you want anything for yourself, you're selfish.

One of the biggest lessons I've learned on my own self-discovery journey, and one of the greatest struggles I see other women having, is that we're walking around following other people's rules, not knowing that we get to decide if they apply to us or not. You may not know it. You probably think the rules are true. You may even think they sound reasonable, but if you are not living a life that you love, you're following rules that are keeping you from creating that life—and you can choose to let them go.

My life mantra has become *I make my own rules.* This mantra was born when I realized that I didn't have to follow other people's rules. I mean, I follow rules. I don't speed or break laws, but when it comes to my life, my choices, and my beliefs, I decide what the rules are. Making your own rules can look different for each person. It might mean that you quit your job to stay home with your kids, or it might mean starting a business or having a career. It might mean traveling the world on your own, traveling the world with your family, or staying in the same place your whole life. It might mean building your ginormous dream house, or selling everything and living in a van down by the river.

Your life. Your rules. You get to decide.

The main purpose of this book is to show you how to do this. You can have whatever you want in life without being a selfish person, and you can do it in your own way.

The Trailblazer Process

In my five-year journey, I've read a lot of books, bought courses, completed trainings, gone to therapy, and worked with life coaches. As I applied all I'd learned to my own life, I noticed a pattern and compiled it all into my three-step Trailblazer process: 1) Find Your Bearings, 2) Follow Your Inner Compass, and 3) Clear Your Path. You must be doing all three steps to truly be a Trailblazer.

21

Find Your Bearings

If you want to become a Trailblazer, it doesn't do you any good to just start creating any new path. You need to pause and Find Your Bearings first. While you may not be happy with the life you're living, truthfully, there's a reason you ended up where you are. Finding Your Bearings asks you to identify how you've been following your Natural Instincts and avoiding your Inner Compass.

It can be hard to know what to change when you don't know where the problem really is. You can try and guess the best solution, but if you don't get to the root of the problem, your solutions will only work temporarily, and no matter how many new solutions you try, you'll end up with the same results. You will save a lot of time, energy, and frustration by taking the time to Find Your Bearings.

To do this, you will take a deeper look at the path you were put on as a child, and question all assumptions regarding your values and beliefs so you can intentionally choose to do something different and stop repeating the same patterns.

Follow Your Inner Compass

Remember, our Inner Compass is the older, wiser part of us—the core of who we are—and living a daring life is the result of learning to trust its guidance. Now that you know your Natural Instincts and your Inner Compass are always battling each other, this part of the journey is learning how to recognize and Trust Your Inner Compass. Being in tune with your Inner Compass is a skill, and it becomes stronger with practice. As you practice, obstacles will make it harder for you to hear the guidance along the way, so it's important to learn how to build a firm foundation for your Inner Compass to thrive and be heard. Not only does your Inner Compass guide you in your choices, but it also guides you to your vision, or your why, and your core values and beliefs. While Finding Your Bearings helps you question your values and beliefs, learning to Trust Your Inner Compass will help you intentionally choose your genuine, authentic values and beliefs.

It's hard to know what the best path for you is when you don't have that Inner Compass to guide you. You may know what is limiting you, or understand why you got to this point in your life and be willing to take action, but if you don't know what you want, you won't know the right action to take. Rather than searching inside, you'll look for someone who has a solution to your problem, and you'll follow their step-by-step map. Their map never fully works, though, because no one else is going to have the perfect map for you. Using that process, you may jump from one guru to the next, hoping in vain to find the perfect map. While you will undoubtedly learn something from these gurus, you'll never feel truly fulfilled until you learn to know and trust your own Inner Compass and find the answer within.

Clear Your Path

Once you've done the work to Find Your Bearings and learned how to Trust Your Inner Compass, you are ready to do the work of taking action and Clearing Your Path. While a lot of Finding Your Bearings and Trusting Your Inner Compass is inner work, Clearing Your Path is the external action. But note: not all action is created equal. Thus, part of Clearing Your Path is learning how to know and do the right actions that will get you to where you want to go.

It's easy to get stuck in the inner work and only think about creating your new path, without moving forward. Reading inspiring quotes, doing research, and learning are helpful, but will only get you so far; taking action is an important part of the process.

Which One Are You?

Do you see where you fall in this process? I don't want you to use this process as a labeling tool, but as more of an awareness tool. If you can see where you fit in this process, it points you to the areas you need to work on the most.

SECTION 2

FIND YOUR BEARINGS

CHAPTER TWO

CHOOSE YOUR OWN ADVENTURE

Finding your bearings starts with your call to adventure. My call was dramatic, in some ways, but quite anticlimactic in the end. Yet, that was what helped me notice it: the lack of drama.

My Call to Adventure

"I need you to stay as still as you can."

I was on a table, about to go into an MRI machine so the tech could take images of my brain. I'd never had to get an MRI before. In fact, I've been exceptionally healthy my whole life. I've never broken any bones, never had to stay in a hospital, and never had to get any x-rays outside of the dentist. I was scared. The fear I felt had a little bit to do with the MRI itself, but mostly I feared the results it could show.

When the tech was ready, she put something resembling a box around my head, and put me into a huge white tube. I'm not typically a claustrophobic person, but I wasn't about to take any chances. I closed my eyes and didn't open them again until I came out. All I remember was a bunch of random, high-pitched sounds, like dolphins having a very spirited conversation, and singing to myself whatever came to mind to keep me calm. As we waited for my results, they set us up in a random, dark closet with a stretcher that I could lie on, because sitting up caused intense, debilitating pain in my head. As I lay there, all I could do was cry. Convinced that I had a brain tumor or cancer and that I didn't have long to live, I thought of my husband and my children. "I'm not ready. I can't leave them. I don't want to go," kept running on repeat through my head.

It was December 2012. I was so excited for Christmas that year because I had planned out a Twenty-Five Days of Christmas calendar of activities, where I had something planned for every day leading up to Christmas. It included crafts, service projects, and fun activities for our family to do together. The first few days had been a success, and we were enjoying ourselves. I decided to take the kids to the movies one day after school. I felt sort of off that morning, but I could still function. I don't even remember what movie we watched because I felt like total crap by the end of it. It was a struggle just to get my kids and me home. When we arrived, I immediately put the TV on for the kids and climbed into my bed. I tried to sleep it off, but I felt worse the next day. It started out as some kind of cold, but it kept getting worse, and no amount of medicine helped. I started getting headaches that continued for days. One morning, I woke up with the worst headache I'd ever had. The light made it worse, which I knew was a symptom of a migraine, but I'd never had a migraine before, so that was strange.

The light sensitivity got so bad my husband eventually had to hang a blanket over the windows and keep all the doors closed so the light couldn't get to me. I couldn't look at screens. I couldn't even sit up without my head feeling like it would explode. At first, my body was so tired I slept most of the day, but eventually, I couldn't fall asleep, so all I could do was lie there in the dark. My thoughts, in the beginning, were positive and hopeful. I'd tell myself that it was OK, that this time would pass and I would get better. But as the days dragged on and my condition worsened, I struggled to stay positive. The hardest part was that I needed so much help. I hated asking other people for help, and I needed help with *everything*. I had people taking my three kids to school, picking them up, and watching them until my husband could pick them up after work. Others were making us dinners. My husband still had to work, then come home and take care of the kids, clean the house, help the kids do homework, etc. I barely saw my kids, because I was so sick and I didn't want to spread it to them in case I was contagious. They would wave to me from the door before leaving for school or say goodnight from the door. I didn't get to hug them, comfort them, or help them.

29

The evenings were the hardest, as I could hear my family living life downstairs without me. I so wanted to be down there with them. My husband is definitely the more patient parent between the two of us, and he had been shouldering the responsibility impressively, so I knew he was overwhelmed when I heard him yelling at a crying child one evening. I don't know the details around the situation; all I know is that I felt completely useless. At that moment, I just sobbed, because not only was I feeling the weight of being sick, but I now felt the weight of the loss that my husband and kids were feeling, as well. It was just as hard for them to not have me around as it was for me to not be around. I went from being positive to having a pity party. "Why is this happening to me? Am I being punished? Is there a lesson I should be learning?" I eventually shifted into hopelessness and defeat, wondering if I was going to die. If my time was up. In those hardest moments, the deep questions came out. "Have I fulfilled my purpose here? Have I accomplished what I wanted to? Have I become the person I want to be?" When I got really honest with myself, I knew the answer to all of them was a big NO. I was trying, and I felt like I was giving my all, but I still didn't feel like I was fulfilling the potential I knew I had within.

One day, I had a straight-up, honest, heart-to-heart talk with God, and after wrestling with my own thoughts, I made a decision. I told him, "OK. If you let me live, I promise I'll dedicate my life to growing and improving myself." I didn't know it then, but that was the moment that changed my life forever. I had finally decided to take control of my life. I'd known for a while that something was missing, but I'd been ignoring it. While I wouldn't want to go through it again, those quiet moments in the dark were a gift.

After things didn't get any better, we decided to go to the doctor. They ran tests but couldn't find anything wrong with me. That's when they ordered the MRI. I got the results back. Nothing!

No tumors. No cancer. No other explanation.

I was relieved, but not really. What the heck was wrong with me? After seeing a neurologist, she gave me a magic pill that made the headaches go away, and within a couple of days, I was better. And we all lived happily ever after.

I'm kidding, but not really. That's what happened.

When I was better and went in for a checkup, I asked my neurologist what had been wrong with me, and she literally shrugged her shoulders. Shrugged her shoulders! She just gave me a pill she thought might work, and luckily, it did. She said it was probably some kind of virus, which just sounds like the doctor version of "I don't know."

Listen, I'm definitely happy I didn't die, but that was kind of a weird and anticlimactic ending to a hugely pivotal moment in my life, don't you think? I've made peace with it by permitting myself to beef up the ending before I tell this story to my future grandkids.

31

The Call to Adventure

In hindsight, while I have no clue what was really wrong with me, I now understand why it happened. The Universe stepped in and gave me a time out. Twice I was given opportunities to change the direction of my life. That letter from my younger self could've been a wake-up call, but I ignored it. Five years after that, I was incredibly unhappy with my life, and I could've used that as a sign that I needed to change direction, but I ignored it and distracted myself by working harder and hustling more. I was willing to do the external work, but I wasn't doing the internal work. Since I wasn't getting it on my own, I needed an intervention. I needed a call to adventure.

I define a call to adventure as a moment that makes you push the pause button on your life. It's a moment where you're forced to change your perspective and be really honest with yourself. My sickness was the first time in my entire life where I was completely stripped of the identity I had built. I'd always seen myself as a high achiever and an independent person. I was the person who went above and beyond in my church duties, volunteered at my kids' school every week, took meals to others, kept my house clean, and cooked homemade meals every night. While none of those things are inherently bad, my reasons for doing them weren't genuine or authentic. I didn't enjoy them. Keeping busy with those tasks was just another way I was fulfilling others' expectations, being a people pleaser, and trying to earn love and acceptance. But when I had my headaches and could only lay there, I was forced to listen to

32

my Inner Compass. I could see that I was doing a lot in my life, but I wasn't doing a lot of what was important to me. I wasn't focusing on the people who meant the most to me: my husband and my kids. What was missing was personal growth. I didn't fully know what I was missing yet, but I did know that if I walked away from my sickness, I was going to figure it out, and I was going to start being more intentional with my life.

Have you heard the song "Live Like You Were Dying" by Tim McGraw? It talks about a man who got a scary health diagnosis and reacted to the news by going skydiving, forgiving people, loving more, and doing what he wanted to do. He re-evaluated his life and did the things that mattered to him. There's nothing like the threat of death to make us look at life in a different way. Suddenly, what seemed really important and necessary isn't even on your radar anymore. Instead, all of your biggest desires, dreams, and aspirations come up, and you find the motivation to do them. Nothing else matters, and you finally go for them because you have nothing to lose.

Couldn't we all look at life this way, though? I mean, technically we're all going to die, so shouldn't we all be thinking about living like we're dying? We get so caught up in distractions that seem really important, yet, if we were going to die tomorrow, how much of them would suddenly be unimportant. What would take top priority? Why are we waiting for a crisis to do those things now?

The truth is, you don't need to wait for a crisis to live the life that you want. Your call to adventure doesn't need to be big or dramatic. It can be as simple as making a decision.

Make a Choice

Did you ever read the *Choose Your Own Adventure* books? I always found them intriguing. As I embarked on the reading adventure, I would read all of the endings first and pick the one I wanted. Then I would read ahead, sift through the different paths, and start making choices. If I didn't like the choice I made, or if I felt that it wasn't going to get me to the ending I wanted, I would go back and find where I'd made the wrong choice and pick the other one. I'd go back and forth like this until I finally reached the ending I wanted. This is likely not how the author intended for the book to be read, but my method works pretty well for making choices in your own real-life adventure.

What if you could look forward to the future and pick the live-like-you-were-dying ending you wanted to get to? What does that ending look like for you?

Now look at where your life is now. Are your choices leading you to the ending you want? What if I told you that you could go back and make a different choice? Not literally, of course. I don't have a DeLorean, Time Turner, or Tardis (if you get any of those references, you're my person and we should be friends). Finding Your Bearings is kind of like going back and figuring out where you made a wrong turn. You can't change the past, but you can identify and understand the choices that led you to your life now so you can choose to do something different and get to your desired ending. Consider this book your call to adventure. Are you willing to take an honest look at the life you've built? At the identity you've built? Are you willing to question it all? This is where you take the first step and the work begins. Let's do this.

CHAPTER THREE

THE WELL-TRAVELED PATH

I remember when the movie *The Matrix* first came out. It blew people's minds, including my own. In one of the most iconic parts of the movie, Morpheus offers his mentee, Neo, a blue pill or a red pill. The blue pill would return him to ignorance. He would go back to not knowing anything else existed outside of the world he knew. The red pill would open his mind and show him the truth, which was that he was living a lie. I remember asking myself which I would choose, the red pill or the blue pill?

I suspect we'd all like to think we'd choose the red pill, and maybe we even believe that our life right now would reflect that choice, but the reality is that most of us took the blue pill a long time ago, and we may not even know it. If you're not happy with your life, and the path you've been put on isn't taking you where you want to go, you chose the blue pill, whether consciously or not.

So why didn't you choose the red pill? What's keeping you from choosing it in your life right now? And how do you move forward?

The Path You're Put on

My therapist loves analogies, and one of her favorites has always stuck with me. Imagine you live in Antarctica. What clothes would you need to survive? Probably lots of layers of shirts, sweaters, a heavy-duty winter coat, gloves, a hat, and maybe a scarf. Now imagine that you decide to move to Hawaii. Do you keep wearing the same clothes? Of course not. You'd die from heat exhaustion. You shed layers. You trade winter coats for tank tops, and winter boots for flip-flops. It makes sense, right? What I needed in Antarctica isn't what I need in Hawaii, so it makes sense that I would get rid of my winter stuff. Except that's not what we do in our lives. Antarctica is our past, and we've been taught what we need to survive there. So, when we move to Hawaii, rather than re-evaluate our new situation and shed the winter clothes, we keep them on and then wonder why we feel like we're slowly dying from heat exhaustion.

Let's take this analogy even deeper. How did I know what was necessary to survive in Antarctica? I've never been there before. I likely learned from a lot of sources: the associate at R.E.I., advice from parents, friends, documentaries, books, and the super cool, adventurous influencer on Instagram.

All the various opinions eagerly fight to get your attention. From birth, we're bombarded with these opinions. We come here with our Natural Instinct as a blank slate. We don't know what it's like to live here. We're pretty helpless, so we need to depend on others for our survival. We start out using our senses to gather information from outside influences. The sights, sounds, and smells give us clues to our surroundings. We pay attention to how others react by noticing their tone of voice and body language. As we start to understand and learn words, we're influenced by what we hear others say. We gather all of this together to form a story in our minds. This story forms the lens through which we see the world around us and our place in it. From this story, we define who we are, what we're capable of, and what's possible for us. We're told what is good and bad, right or wrong, beautiful and ugly, normal and weird.

And none of it is really our choice. Children get to make very few choices; they don't get to choose their name, what language they speak, or what religion they're raised in. Because they need their parents to survive, they have to trust them, so whatever their parents teach them, they believe without question. So, back to the analogy, our trusted advisors basically give us a list of winter gear, and we just get what they say. If my parents say I need a rubber ducky in Antarctica, I'm going to get that rubber ducky.

We don't consciously know that we're agreeing to this, but we are.

39

Fast forward to moving to Hawaii, A.K.A adulthood. If you're adhering to the same things you were taught as a child, that's the equivalent of keeping your winter gear on. That uncomfortable feeling, the heat exhaustion, is a sign that you have some beliefs, values, or limitations that you have been taught but no longer need or want. Perhaps it's time to trade in some ski goggles for some sunglasses.

So why is this important to know? Because if you don't know that your beliefs have been taught to you, you just assume that they *are* you. And if you're feeling out of alignment, it will be confusing. You won't know what the right choices are. You may also think there's something wrong with you, or you're doing something wrong when, in reality, the story you were taught is shaping how you see both yourself and the world. It's also influencing the actions you take and, therefore, creating the results in your life. It's OK to question all your values and beliefs—and it's actually not a big deal to do so—because you never really chose them to begin with.

When I wrote that letter to my future self as a teenager, I thought I had chosen my own path by being daring and honest enough to write my true dreams in that letter. This declaration that was seen by no one besides me for five years was a start, but it wasn't enough to get me where I wanted to go. If I wanted to walk the path I'd declared in my letter, I would need to first become consciously aware of the path I'd been placed on and intentionally step off onto a new one.

That sounds like no big deal, but if it wasn't a big deal, more women would be doing it. So what keeps us from stepping off the path we've been put on?

Reason #1: Fear of Losing Something

We all like rewards. We live in a society that has trained us from childhood to believe that we'll be rewarded if we do something "good." When we get good grades, we get praised by our parents and teachers. When we do our chores, we get to watch TV. When we do what our parents say, we're a "good girl." When we don't do exactly what we're told, we lose those rewards. Thus, when we step off the path, we fear we'll lose our "perfect" image or reputation, someone won't like us anymore, or a loved one might grow angry and cut off ties.

Reason #2: Fear of Punishment

Another consequence of not doing what we're told is punishment. We might be grounded, get spanked, have to do extra chores, or maybe our punishment is verbal, such as name-calling, being shamed, or being told we were a "bad girl." As an adult, that can look like the silent treatment from someone we love, criticism about our character, or being yelled at.

41

Reason #3: It's Easier

Any time we walk against a strong force, such as walking upstream or walking against the wind, it will be harder. If given a choice, we humans like to take the easier path. Questioning or going against the ones we love or the majority is harder than just going with the crowd, where we get less resistance and we don't have to deal with the negative responses.

While these three things may explain why you're not questioning the path you've been put on, the reality is what you're afraid of is already happening in your life.

You fear that you'll lose something or someone you love, but what you don't realize is that every time you take a step toward a path you don't want but choose just to make other people happy, you take a step away from your true, authentic self. You're already losing yourself.

You're afraid of punishment from others, but what you don't realize is that, by trying to make other people happy, you've now formed an ideal you that you're constantly trying to live up to, even though perfection is impossible. When you don't live up to that standard, you get angry and disappointed in yourself, which may result in negative self-talk, disconnecting from others, emotional eating, or other unhelpful behaviors. No one has to punish you. You're already punishing yourself.

It seems easier to avoid confrontation by doing what others want you to do. It seems easier to go with the crowd because you don't have to deal with the negativity. Except, then you start feeling bitterness and resentment that you have to do things the way other people want you to. They don't know you're upset, but you do. You feel it. You are making their life easier and your life harder.

So How Do You Change This?

Question It All

If this is the first time you've ever been introduced to the idea that within your consciousness there is the Natural Instinct and the Inner Compass, your first question may be, "How do I know the difference?" How do I distinguish the path I've been put on from what my Inner Compass is telling me? It's a valid question. The first thing you can do to take a step off the path is to question all of your assumptions. In the beginning, you may not know the difference between your Natural Instinct and Inner Compass, so by questioning everything, you can start sorting it out one-by-one.

Remember, Finding Your Bearings is all about understanding how you got to where you are, so keep an open mind as you move forward. If you're feeling a little defensive or uncomfortable at the thought of questioning everything, let me be clear: I'm not saying you have to give up all your beliefs.

43

Questioning doesn't equal giving up. It just means re-evaluate or reconsider. And if you still believe something, then you will now know that you chose it and aren't just going along with what someone else chose for you—and that will make a huge difference.

Choose the Red Pill

It can be a harsh truth to realize you didn't choose the subconscious story that's been influencing your life, but I hope you realize how freeing it can be, too. By exposing the real problem, you can choose something different, and have a real chance at creating what you want. For possibly the first time in your life, you will have the opportunity to choose your critical values and beliefs. You get to choose. Isn't that so empowering?

Looking back, I can identify many times I felt this inner struggle, and what I now realize is, in these moments, my Inner Compass was trying to tell me that something wasn't aligned. It was trying to offer me the red pill, but I chose the safer thing. I chose the blue pill, and continued on living as before. It wasn't until after my sickness that I saw the opportunity for what it was, and for the first time, I started seeing my life from a new perspective. By questioning everything, I could make sustainable and powerful changes in my life. This is your moment to decide. Will you continue on as you did before, or start fully stepping into your power and take your life back?

44

Self-Reflection

1. Can you identify the story that others taught you? Write down anything that comes to mind automatically.

2. Can you think of choices you've made where you felt a pull between your Natural Instinct and your Inner Compass?

3. While questioning everything, did you find any beliefs that don't align with your Inner Compass?

CHAPTER FOUR

FEAR

I have a confession to make: I'm a big scaredy-cat. My Natural Instinct has inspired me to be extremely paranoid, and listening to it always conjures up visions of the worst-case scenarios in all situations of my life. I jump and scream at the littlest things. While I try not to live in fear, I admit that fear has stopped me from pursuing dreams in the past, and kept me stuck in unhappiness for years.

But it doesn't have to be that way for us. The biggest problem with fear is that we don't understand it. While fear has its downsides, it's actually not all bad. There's a purpose for it. The problem is not in the feeling itself, it's that we don't understand its purpose, so we give it more power than it needs to have. Let's start by understanding the real purpose of fear, and then identify whether you're using it to your advantage or disadvantage.

Tigers and Mean Girls

Back during the time of our early ancestors, they had to be aware of many physical threats, like tigers. If a tiger chased you and you didn't run away or (try to) fight it, you would die. That's not good. For your survival, fear kicks in when you see that tiger. Your body responds by initiating the fight or flight mode, and you get a rush of adrenaline to help you fight for your life. This is fear's good side. It's called physical fear.

Now imagine that you sign up for a painting class because you want to learn to paint. You drive to the class and sit in your car, paralyzed with fear. You're scared that you'll fail, or that people will make fun of your painting. You're not even sure that you're capable of doing it. You take your concerns in as truth and let your fear talk you out of going in. Instead, you drive home to watch Bob Ross masterfully paint his happy trees from the comfort of your own home.

Is this physical fear? Will you literally die if someone makes fun of your painting? Will you die if you fail to be Bob Ross from the first stroke of the brush? No. And this is where the problem lies. We don't question these fearful thoughts that our brain offers us; we just accept them as truth. This is the ugly side of fear. This is called psychological fear, and it's created by your thoughts, not by a real physical threat.

I got the term "Tigers and Mean Girls" from my first life coach. It was a fun and short way to remind myself that not all fear is deadly. When I was afraid, I would ask myself, "Is this a tiger or a mean girl?" If it was a tiger, then the fear was legitimate and I could decide what to do from there. If it was a mean girl, I would either dismiss it, get curious about it, or try to reframe it and change my perspective. Most of the time I find that my fears are just mean girls. They aren't real, physical threats. If you start asking yourself this simple question when you feel fear, I'm betting you'll find that this is the case for you.

Why Is This Important?

If you want to be a Trailblazer, you're going to have to recognize the difference between tigers and mean girls. Doing something new will always trigger fear, so recognizing whether your fear is helping you stay alive or limiting you will determine your ability to create your new path. If it's not literally keeping you safe, fear is not useful. Fear will never fully go away, but the better you get at recognizing it, the quicker you will be able to move forward in your life.

The #1 Fear

Do you know what people's #1 fear is? Many say it's the fear of failure, but it's not—it's the fear of *success*. That doesn't sound right, does it? What could possibly be scary about success?

We're scared to succeed, because if we can succeed at one thing, that means we can succeed at other things—which means anything is possible. Your Natural Instinct causes you to dislike the idea that anything is possible, because that means you would have to take responsibility for your own life adventure. It would mean you can no longer make excuses. It would mean that, if you aren't succeeding, you can only blame yourself.

This also shows up when we hear of others' success. Recently, a woman tried to share her excitement about positive changes in her life with her friends and was surprised when her friends responded negatively. They could barely stand her even talking about some of the things she'd been learning about herself. For the life of her, she couldn't understand why others weren't as excited as she was.

Most people don't want to know that they can take control and make changes in their lives. They want to stay ignorant because they know, deep down, that if they acknowledge that change is possible, that means they have to do something. They can no longer make excuses for why they aren't living their dreams. Instead, they would have to stop blaming life circumstances or other people. Thus, they would realize they are the reason they aren't getting their desired results. And that is too scary, so they avoid it altogether.

Your Natural Instinct won't come out and tell you that you're afraid of success. It will come up with a lot of excuses and reasons why you aren't living your dreams. And, believe me, they'll sound reasonable:

I don't want to leave people behind.
My children are my first priority, as they should be.
I don't need money to be happy.
I just need a moment to stop thinking.
I'll have time for my dreams later.
It's selfish to want more than you have.
I don't need self-help stuff. I'm fine without it.

All of these beliefs are meant to keep you small. While they sound reasonable, they have deeper implications that are rooted in fear.

The Natural Instinct will make it seem like a bad thing that you no longer have to depend on other people to be happy, but you can change that perspective. If anything was truly possible and you didn't need to depend on anyone else to make things happen, what kind of life could you have? You would be unstoppable. If you can truly embrace success, rather than fear it, you will be able to conquer all the other fears that get in your way. Your success will be inevitable.

Self-Reflection

1. Write down your greatest fears. Are they tigers or mean girls? Question them, and ask yourself whether these fears are useful or if they're holding you back in some way.

2. Are you afraid of success? How might it be showing up in your life?

CHAPTER FIVE

THE NATURAL INSTINCT

When I was a little girl, my parents enrolled me in a gymnastics class. I very vividly remember my outfit, which consisted of a hot pink Little Mermaid leotard (my favorite Disney movie growing up) and bright blue leggings. The leotard was sleeveless, with pink ruffles at the shoulders. My parents would have had a hard time losing me in a crowd, with those bright colors, but I felt like a rock star.

It took me a while to warm up to the idea of trying new things in front of other people. The fear of failure was very strong for me, even at that young age. With time, though, I started to get more confident (my outfit helped). I enjoyed the challenge and loved seeing my progress. Eventually, I reached the age where you had to decide between going competitive or stopping. I remember the moment my mom asked me whether I wanted to go competitive. While trying to decide, I may have been quiet on the outside, but a lot was going on in my mind. Part of me wanted to continue. I loved gymnastics. I could see myself working hard and becoming really good at it, but then the other part of me had watched the competitive coaches working with the older girls, and they didn't seem very nice. They were stricter. They never smiled. The gymnasts were challenged more, and had to learn more complicated techniques and skills. Self-doubt crept in. I was scared I couldn't keep up. What if I failed? What if my coaches yelled at me? What if they kicked me out because I wasn't good enough? I thought about my family. It would likely cost a lot more money to keep going. I told myself I would have to be really good if my parents spent that money on me. After all, if I couldn't compete, I would've wasted all of their money. I was just a little girl, but I was already aware that everything costs money, and that we didn't exactly have an overabundance of it. If they spent the money on me, there would be less for the rest of my family. That pressure, along with the fear of increased expectations from the coaches, influenced my final decision. I told my mom I didn't want to keep going. Even as the words were coming out of my mouth, I felt regret. I wanted to stay, so why was I choosing to stop?

This wasn't the only time my Natural Instinct kicked in and I made a self-destructive choice. If I'd known then how to recognize my Natural Instinct, my life would've turned out very differently. I don't regret it, because I believe we have our experiences for a reason, but the problem was that I was still being led by my Natural Instinct in adulthood. I needed to break the pattern that had started from a very young age. While your Natural Instinct may be showing up in your life in many ways, I will focus on these five:

1. How you see your past

2. Trying to fit in

3. How you see yourself

4. Limiting beliefs

5. Indecisiveness

1. How you see your past

Your Natural Instinct leads you to focus on the past. Because your Natural Instinct exists to ensure your survival, you use the past to determine what is possible for you now and in the future, when you're operating under its influence. It doesn't allow you to believe that anything is possible in the future, because you can't plan for that. Have you ever thought to try something new, just to be reminded of the times you failed, so you decide you won't try? Maybe you dreamed of leaving your hometown and traveling the world, but you remind yourself that no one in your family has ever left this town. Next thing you know, you resign yourself to watching other people travel on Instagram, or pin beautiful travel locations on Pinterest. Or maybe you dreamed of owning a business or having a career, but then you remember that your mom sacrificed her dreams to raise you, so you should stay home and raise your kids, too. Neither of these scenarios, or any other scenario, is inherently a problem. The problem is your Natural Instinct uses your past to stop you from going after your desires.

Your Natural Instinct exists to help you. But the real truth is that it's limiting you. Anytime you're using your past as an excuse, you need to dig deeper. I don't usually see very much value in using your past, as you go on to make choices in the present or future. I do think there's value in using it as you Find Your Bearings, because your past is where you're going to uncover what's holding you back. So, how can you use your past in a helpful way?

If someone was making a movie of your life, what would you characterize it as? A tragedy? A comedy? A drama?

What role would you play in your life movie? The supporting actor? The villain? The damsel in distress?

How you see your past and the role you play in it affects the life you're creating right now and how you show up in it. If you think your life is a tragedy, you'll attract more opportunities for tragedy. If you think your life is a drama, you'll attract more drama into your life. If you think your life is a comedy, you won't take it seriously, and, therefore, will attract others who don't take you seriously.

If you believe you're the supporting actor, you're going to show up by supporting the people around you. You're not going to see your dreams, your wants, or your needs as a priority, nor will you see yourself as important as the "main characters." You may use your past as evidence that you're not capable or deserving of your dreams, that other people get to have what they want.

If you believe that you're the villain, you're going to see yourself as the bad guy. Maybe you think no one likes you, and you're the one to blame for the problems that arise in everyone else's life. You likely don't think very highly of yourself, and feel a lot of shame for who you are. You may use your past as evidence that no one understands you, they don't love you for who you are, or you're not lovable. You see your differences as bad, especially if you've received negative responses from other people because of them.

If you believe that you're the damsel in distress, you're going to wait for someone to come and fix all the problems, to come and save you. You'll be waiting for your hero. You may use the lack of a hero in your past as an excuse for not accomplishing your goals and dreams. You don't think you're capable of getting what you want on your own. You likely have a lot of gurus, mentors, or people that you admire and follow to inspire you and show you how to be happier. If their methods don't work for you, you blame it on their method. You may also look back and see all the ways that people didn't step up for you, and it probably affects your relationships with those people.

See what I mean? If any of these resonate with you, I'm going to offer you a new story and role right now. What if you were the hero? Everyone loves an underdog story where the unlikely hero starts from nothing, rises to the challenge, learns and grows, and saves everyone in the end. What if that was your story?

If you're thinking that you couldn't possibly be the hero, think about this: in 1400s France, Joan of Arc was a peasant girl, born to a farmer. She couldn't read or write, but her mother was very religious and taught her about her faith. By many standards, she would be considered quite unextraordinary. At the age of thirteen, Joan heard voices, which she attributed to angels, telling her that she needed to help save France from falling into the hands of English rule. At that time, England and France were in the midst of the Hundred Years' War, fighting over who would rule France. Before Joan came along, it was not looking good for the French. Joan convinced the French king to allow her to lead an army to Orleans. This was a young girl with no military training or background. Who knew that, in the end, she would play such a pivotal role in France's victory over England? Joan could have easily dismissed her visions and stayed in the French village where she had a safe, predictable life, but she had heard her call to adventure, to a greater purpose, and she chose to follow it. Her path was filled with trials. It took several attempts just to figure out how to get an audience with the king and find safe travel to him. She was injured several times in battle, and eventually she was captured by England and burned at the stake. I'm sure many times she felt scared. Perhaps she even doubted in her abilities, though it doesn't seem that her trust in God ever wavered. I'm sure she had many who doubted her visions, doubted in her ability as a woman in battle (and a young woman, at that). Yet, she never gave up. She stayed true to herself and what she believed, even when others didn't believe her and she was sentenced to death. She started out in humble beginnings, but she didn't let that hold her back from fulfilling her purpose and growing into a hero. While she lived a short life, she made an impact, and is seen as a hero, even now, centuries later.

Why can't that be you? All of our journeys will be different, but this is the story of all Trailblazers. If you can see your past as a hero's journey, you will look at it differently. You won't let humble beginnings or struggles determine what you're capable of, because all of the best heroes start in humble circumstances, don't they? In fact, it's their humble circumstances that helped them grow and become who they are. Trailblazers look at their trials and setbacks as the experiences that shape their character.

Often, the hardest moments in life help create the parts about you that you love the most. As a child, I was labeled as sensitive and emotional. I feel emotions very strongly, and when I do, I cry. Not just when I'm sad, but also when I'm scared, tired, happy, surprised, and angry. This is just how my body reacts to the strong emotions that I feel. When I was younger, I felt a lot of shame because I got teased or punished for it. I would try to control it, but I was never able to, which just resulted in me feeling more shame. I thought it meant that I was weak. Through my own journey, I've learned to see my emotion differently.

My ability to feel emotion deeply makes it very easy for me to connect with others and understand how they feel. I intuitively can tell when someone needs help, and I often know how to help them. It has helped me become a caring, compassionate, and empathetic person—and I love that about myself. I no longer look at my emotion as a weakness, I see it as a strength.

The great thing about an underdog story or an unlikely hero is that their journey can start at any time. You can choose to be the hero in your hero's journey right now. Everything before this moment is your humble beginning. This book is your call to rise to the challenge of creating a fulfilling and purposeful life, and you can intentionally start making those steps now.

Self-Reflection:

1. Look at your life as an underdog story. What were your humble beginnings? What are the things that could hold you back from reaching your potential?

2. As the unlikely hero, what have you gone through that has prepared you for your hero role?

2. Trying to fit in

When I was a teenager, I looked up to an older girl named Crystal in my church group. I looked up to all the older girls in our youth group, but Crystal always stood out to me because she was different. She was nice to everyone, especially the younger girls. She never was too cool, and was always willing to take us under her wing. But above all else, she wasn't afraid to be herself. She had a confidence about her that didn't seem to be dependent on what others thought of her. She was unapologetic about who she was, and wasn't afraid to take up space with her opinions or her presence. She intrigued me. When I was a sophomore in high school, Crystal died in a car accident. Her death impacted me greatly. Death is always sad, but something about Crystal's death specifically left a void in my life. At fifteen years old, I couldn't put it into words, but as I've thought about her throughout the years, I can see it now. Crystal was the first person in my life who didn't care about fitting in. She wasn't afraid to break the "rules." She didn't care about being cool, or feel like she had to do things like everyone else did. And when I was around her, I felt like maybe I could do that, too.

Our Natural Instinct cares about fitting in. It believes that fitting in is vital to survival, because our early ancestors' survival was dependent on belonging to a group. Listening to this part of your Natural Instinct manifests as people-pleasing, where you are trying to make those around you happy. Your choices are dependent on how others react, and you are

61

constantly looking for the approval of others. Often, if you are listening to your Natural Instinct in this way in one area of your life, you are likely doing it in others. It can show up in your relationships with family, co-workers, your boss, friends, church, or even strangers.

The problem with trying to fit in is that it leads to you being dependent on other people for your happiness. If your thoughts create your reality, then the truth is that other people's thoughts create their reality. This means you have no control over what people think or feel about you, yet you act as if you do by choosing to do things to influence how they're thinking or feeling. When you believe that you can influence their thoughts about you, you will constantly hustle for their approval, and the hustle never ends. It's not only exhausting, but you can feel really defeated when you try to make someone happy and they still choose not to be.

The alternative is to look at your life from the inside. You do things because they're aligned with who you want to be. For example, maybe you call your mom every week, but rather than doing it from obligation or because you think she'll get mad if you don't, you do it because you love her and that is how you want to express it. Do you see the difference? In the first example, you could call your mom and she could still choose to be mad at you, leaving you feeling confused and maybe upset. The second option allows you to feel love, regardless of how your mom chooses to feel. By looking within yourself for validation, you no longer have to hustle for it from others.

Crystal was my first example of living life like this. She knew who she was and she wasn't afraid to live her life the way she wanted. My last memory of her was a moment after one of the weekly youth activities for our church. The activity ended early, but rather than heading home, she asked me if I wanted to hang out for a little bit longer. She bought me a Slurpee, and we went back to her house, where we talked and laughed in her room. I don't remember what we talked about, but I do remember the feeling I felt. I felt accepted. She liked me, but not because I was doing anything. She liked me just for being me, just as she liked herself for just being her. Her life here on this Earth was short, but even all these years later, I've never forgotten the influence that she had on me. As I think of her, she continues to show me the impact one person can have just by being themself.

Self-Reflection:

1. How are you living your life? Are you trying to fit in?

2. Are you looking outside of yourself for validation, or basing your choices on how others may react?

3. What would it mean for you to show up as who you want to be?

3. How you see yourself

As a self-protection mechanism, I learned at a very young age that, if you put up a tough exterior, you hurt less. It worked pretty well at keeping the haters out, but I was so focused on keeping people out, I trapped myself in with the meanest person I've ever known. My inner mean girl. While I put on this outer air of confidence, inside I hardly had a nice thing to say about myself.

I saw myself as weak because I couldn't control my emotions. I didn't think I was pretty enough because I didn't look like all the other girls around me. I didn't think I was talented because I wasn't on a sports team and didn't have any particular skill that made me stand out. If I ever performed anything less than perfectly, my inner mean girl was there, telling me I was stupid, that I never did anything right, and that I was never good enough.

I know I'm not the only one with an inner mean girl. How did she come to be, and why is she so mean?

Remember that path we're put on? Our inner mean girl comes from there. As we walk down this path that others have made for us, that path becomes our truth. While we first start out walking because the influences around us tell us to, it becomes so ingrained in us that we eventually don't need them to tell us to keep walking. We walk on our own. Through the story we've made out of all the information we've gathered from outside expectations, we've formed an image of what it means to be a

64

"good girl," or, later in life, an image of what being "enough" looks like. This image becomes our standard, and every time we don't live up to it, we reject ourselves. We get frustrated for not being perfect, and our inner mean girl comes out and punishes us for our imperfection. Our Natural Instinct leads to this behavior because it's trying to inspire you to change. It doesn't work, though, because shame doesn't inspire change; it just makes you want to hide.

Unfortunately, if you don't know the difference between your Inner Compass and your Natural Instinct, you think your inner mean girl is you, making it difficult to love yourself. We often hear our thoughts spoken in our voice, so we just believe that whatever we hear is truth, and we don't question the thoughts. However, by separating your Natural Instinct voice from your Inner Compass, you can identify the image of perfection you've created, question it, and release it. When you're able to recognize that negative self-talk is not truth, and not your Inner Compass talking, you can dismiss your inner mean girl and choose to intentionally think thoughts that will help you feel love for yourself.

Self-Reflection:

1. What does your inner mean girl say to you?

2. Question those thoughts. Are they true? Do they help you be who you want to be?

4. Limiting beliefs

A belief is an acceptance that something is true. How do our beliefs form? They form when we think a thought many times. In other words, beliefs are formed through repetition. As we're gathering outside information and forming our story, we're going to pay closer attention to the messages we keep hearing over and over. Most of our beliefs will start in childhood, in the home we grew up in, but they can also come from other sources such as media, school, peers, or church. Because these limiting beliefs form in our childhood, most of us aren't conscious of them. If we don't take the time to question and intentionally decide what we want to believe, we just continue to carry the beliefs that were conditioned into us as children.

It's not a matter of whether you have limiting beliefs, it's a matter of what they are. We all have them. Most people don't recognize how powerful words are, so they don't pay attention to what they're saying, or the effect it could have. For example, "Money doesn't grow on trees" implies scarcity and a lack of abundance. This thought can cause you to feel resentment toward those who have more money than you, because their abundance means there's less money out there for you. This is not true, but this limiting belief reinforced many times will form your story about money and will affect your experiences with it. Whether intentionally or not, these limiting beliefs are passed down to us and contribute to the reality we are creating. Rather than holding on to these limiting beliefs, you can question their truthfulness and usefulness, then choose to let them go and think more helpful thoughts.

Self-Reflection:

1. What areas in your life feel unfulfilled, and what limiting beliefs have contributed to that?

2. What are the excuses that your brain gives you? These answers can give you clues about what your limiting beliefs might be.

5. Indecisiveness

Have you ever had to make a decision and you didn't know what to choose, so you just stood there, paralyzed? Indecisiveness often happens when you're trying to decide between two values. You may be having an internal battle between what you really value and what you've been conditioned to value. Or you may not be clear about what your values really are, so you genuinely don't know which one you prize more.

Values can be conditioned in us, just like our limiting beliefs. Our parents teach us what they value, and those priorities become ours, too. But as you get older, you may find that your values differ from what you've been taught. If you aren't aware that you have conditioned values, you won't know why you feel this inner battle. An easy way to identify the core values you were taught is to pay attention to what you think you "should" do. "I should do this," or "I should want this." The thought "I want *this*, but I should want *that*" is a clue that you are struggling between what you want and what you've been taught to want. As you become aware of your conditioned core values, you can evaluate them and decide if you want to keep them or let them go.

If you've already done the work of evaluating and letting go, but you still feel unfulfilled, the struggle may come from the fact that you don't know what you value. You've let go of the values that aren't important to you, but have you gone through and decided what you *do* value? It's just as important to get clear about what you value. Once you've done that, you'll be able to make decisions much more quickly. Decisions become easy when you know what's important to you and you know who you're trying to be.

Self-Reflection:

1. What are the values that you have been taught? If you're not sure, think of all the things you think you "should" do or be. Do you genuinely value these things?

2. What do you value?

Being aware of how your Natural Instinct is showing up in your life is one method to identify ways you're staying stuck, but that's not enough by itself. The next step is identifying how you're avoiding your Inner Compass.

CHAPTER SIX

AVOIDING YOUR INNER COMPASS

Before my mystery sickness, I had an inner feeling that kept nagging at me. I wanted more in my life. I saw that desire as evidence that I was ungrateful, or that something was wrong with me.

What I came to realize is that the feeling was not nagging *at* me . . . it was calling *to* me.

It was a call to my true self.

I realize now that, as much as I was blindly following my Natural Instinct, I was equally avoiding my Inner Compass because it contradicted the people around me. I didn't want to listen because I didn't want to be different. Different was scary. And lonely.

There are three ways people avoid their Inner Compass: deny/ignore, misunderstand, and hide/distract. Let's take a look at each of these, and then I'll introduce you to a better alternative—surrender.

Deny/Ignore

If you deny or ignore your Inner Compass, you resist what your authentic self is telling you and ignore the feeling that something is not quite right. You subconsciously try to prove your Inner Compass wrong by doing anything and everything *except* for what you know deep down is right for you. The feeling that something isn't quite right, a feeling of misalignment, is with you always.

In other words, you know what you feel called to do, but it's scary or hard, so you resist it. You continue to believe life is something that is happening *to* you because that feels safer than taking control of your life.

Misunderstand

If you misunderstand the Inner Compass, you think the call for more means that you need something more outside of you. Rather than looking inward and seeking the answers within you, you look for gurus/mentors, friends, or family to tell you what to do. It's believing that a perfect answer is *out there* that you need to find, rather than understanding that the best answer is already *within you.*

AVOIDING YOUR INNER COMPASS

Hide/Distract

If you distract yourself whenever you feel that Inner Compass, you'll feel uncomfortable, and you'll try to hide from it. My personal distraction of choice is french fries and a Diet Coke. For you, this may look like chocolate, alcohol, social media, binge-watching Netflix, or staying busy. By keeping yourself busy or distracted with all the options out there, you don't have to pay attention to that Inner Compass.

Surrender

You recognize the Inner Compass for what it is: a warning that you're out of alignment. You don't make it mean that everything is going wrong, or that there's something wrong with you. It's just a sign that you need to look at what you're doing and re-evaluate it. It may require a big change or a little change. There's no way of knowing, at this stage, but you're willing to surrender to the call and dig a little deeper.

Self-Reflection:

1. Can you identify ways where you have been avoiding your Inner Compass? If so, how?

73

The first three reactions—deny/ignore, misunderstand, and hide/distract—are all efforts to avoid the Inner Compass, while the fourth one, surrender, is about embracing it.

If you look at the Inner Compass as a negative thing, you'll try not to feel it. The problem with that is that you can't escape it. It will always be there until you address it. Choosing one of the first three is easier in the short run, but, in the long run, it's harder because you're constantly in pursuit of quieting the call. This results in prolonged suffering because you stay stuck.

When you choose to see the Inner Compass as a positive thing, you embrace it rather than avoid it. You can check in with yourself, decide what you want, and move forward much more quickly. This is not to say that doing the inner work is easy. The up-front work is hard because it requires making decisions and taking action, but it will also lead to joy, peace, and fulfillment.

So where do you stand? What are your actions telling you? If you've been avoiding your Inner Compass, don't feel bad. We all do it. Even after years of working on this myself, I still, more often than not, react in one of the first three ways, initially. The key is to know that we all have to move to surrender before we can truly tap into our Inner Compass. While, after years of practice, I sometimes can move straight to surrender, the biggest difference between where I started and where I am now is that I now recognize when I'm keeping myself stuck, and I surrender a lot faster. The goal is not to get to a point where we avoid reacting negatively at all—we are imperfect humans, after all—but to move ourselves to surrender in less time than it took before.

Before we move on, let's talk about the word *surrender* for a moment. Sometimes words themselves can tell a story, and surrender often has a negative connotation. It implies that you've submitted, lost, given up, or stopped resisting or fighting. And while that is exactly what I'm talking about, I want you to look at it in a more empowering way.

The truth is that you're already surrendering your life. You're surrendering to your Natural Instinct by accepting life as it comes to you, with no control. You're giving in to the expectations of others, rather than deciding what you want. You're giving in to your past and letting it decide what you're capable of in your future.

What I'm asking you to do is to stop surrendering to your Natural Instinct and start surrendering to your Inner Compass instead.

I want you to stop surrendering to what's easy and start surrendering to the more fulfilling work.

I want you to stop surrendering to the limitations in your head and start surrendering to the authentic part of you that wants to come out.

Now that you understand what's gotten you to where you are now, it's time to learn how to trust the part of you that will lead you to where you want to go—your Inner Compass.

SECTION 3

FOLLOW YOUR INNER COMPASS

CHAPTER SEVEN

STEPPING INTO THE UNKNOWN

"I assumed that people were sucking on purpose, just to piss me off . . ."

"Holy crap. This woman is reading my mind. That's exactly how I feel," I said to myself, as I watched a video on boundaries from a woman named Brené Brown.

I had been mindlessly scrolling Facebook, trying to escape the crappiness of my life, when, for some reason, I decided to watch a video my friend had shared. I don't really believe in love at first sight, but with Brené, in that moment . . . well, I'm not sure it could be described as anything else. I was shocked at how this woman, whom I'd never seen or heard of before, could sum up everything I was feeling in one sentence. My husband and I had just adopted our daughter. I learned a lot about myself through the process, and my marriage was strengthened. But, while the adoption journey up to this point was a beautiful experience, I was now feeling alone in my feelings. One of the biggest warnings you get as an adoptive parent is you'll need to identify common struggles and know how to help the adoptive child adjust. I put all of my focus on being prepared for any emotional or behavioral struggles that might come up for her. Bringing our daughter home for the first time was special and unforgettable. She fit in almost effortlessly. Turns out that the part I was most worried about ended up being the easiest. The adoption books are really good at preparing you for your child, but what they don't do well is prepare you for all the other problems that might come up because of this big life change. It was the people around me that sucked, not the issues from my adoptive daughter. I was living a paradox: I saw adoption as a blessing in my life, as it brought me a lot of joy, yet it was also the reason I was dealing with these other struggles that resulted in my anger and unhappiness. In that moment, as I heard Brené say those words, I felt like she understood me better than any other person in my life. It was the first glimmer of hope that I'd felt in a while. A small spark of light in an ongoing darkness.

The next spark of light was going to therapy. A few years ago, my friend had mentioned I should try therapy. We were talking on the phone, and I'd been venting all my problems to her. The bitterness and anger in my words and tone couldn't be denied. I knew they were at an unhealthy level, but I was doing everything I could think of. I was seriously at a loss as to why nothing was working. She had been going to couples therapy for a few months and suggested that it might be helpful for me. I immediately went from "everything is horrible" to "I'm fine" in the blink of an eye. I felt something telling me I should go, but I wasn't willing to acknowledge that feeling, and I buried it deep down.

You see, from a very young age, I learned to depend on myself. My job, my mission, was to be the least amount of a burden as possible. I got a job as early as I could, and paid for as much as I could with my own money. Emotionally, I just dealt with my own stuff—and by dealt, I mean I wrote/vented in my journal and stuffed my feelings deep down. But, hey, I was surviving, in my mind. I didn't like asking for help or depending on anyone else to help me, and only did so in very dire circumstances. That's why I shut down the idea of going to therapy. I told myself that I didn't need it, that I could do it on my own. All I really needed to do was pray more and have more faith.

That didn't work.

I just kept getting angrier and angrier, not to mention bitter, as time went on. Now the adoption had brought up a lot of unforeseen baggage. Our classes hadn't prepared us for the other muck that it brought up, mainly our relationships with other people. I was blindsided by it all. I told you how I hated asking for help, right? We were very honest and straightforward with the people I thought would be our greatest supporters, and we told them what our greatest needs would be, moving forward. But when we really needed them, they weren't there. I felt so betrayed. To me, it was more evidence that people can't be trusted. It was the ultimate evidence that people sucked.

During our last meeting with our social worker, I was telling her what was happening, and after she patiently heard me out, she said, "I think you should see a therapist." Strike two.

I immediately started crying. I knew she was right, but I refused to fully accept it. I knew a lot of people went to therapy, but no one in my world had ever done it, that I knew of.

In my mind, going to therapy meant admitting I couldn't do it alone, and that I needed someone else to get me through it. Going to therapy implied that something was wrong with me, and everyone would know it. Our social worker gave me the therapist's info and left. I intended to call, but never actually did. I would often have these up and down moments. In the up moments, I got a hold of my anger and had better days. It felt like I had a handle on the situation. And then something would happen that would send me into a down moment, and any progress that I'd made would be lost, and then some. In those moments, I would always feel that inner nudge to therapy, but I'd brush it off and just resolve to try harder.

Strike three, or the breaking point, came when we had some people visiting us. I'd just gone through an up moment, so I thought I was in a good place and could handle it.

I had a full-on breakdown.

Like a hyperventilating, sobbing, hot mess sort of breakdown.

In that moment, my husband compassionately told me, "I don't know how to help you."

And that was the moment.

In that raw, vulnerable state, my husband saying those words didn't break me, but when I repeated those words to myself, I finally had to admit that I *didn't know how to help me*. I had to admit to myself that I couldn't do it on my own this time.

I knew what path I needed to take. It was the right path, all along; it just took me a long time, and a lot of unnecessary suffering, to finally stop denying it. It was scary because it was new. No one I knew had taken this path before. I didn't know what it would look like, but I knew I was being called to this. And I was finally ready to accept it.

Leap of Faith

Any time you try to change routine, your Natural Instinct will show up in the form of resistance. Why? Because something new is unpredictable, and survival is harder when you don't have data to help you make the safest decision. Knowing that your Natural Instincts will show up in this way will help you recognize it when it happens, which allows you to not just blindly give in to it.

I was so nervous for my first session of therapy. I didn't have any knowledge of psychology, so therapy seemed like a very out-there concept. I had no clue what it would be like. At the end of my first session, my therapist explained that we'd be using EMDR therapy to go through my past. I didn't know if it was going to work. I can tell you, as I told her, that I was skeptical, but I was also desperate. I refused to stay stuck any longer, and if I had to do nontraditional stuff to move forward, I would do it. It makes me laugh now because EMDR therapy is really not that weird. And if my past self saw the spiritual things that I learn, study, and practice now, she probably wouldn't believe that I was the future version of her. I'm so different, she'd find it hard to see the possibility of being where I am now. While that's mind-blowing to think about, it is a good thing. It means I made some big changes. I used a lot of energy trying to plan out what therapy would look like for me, and in the end, it didn't turn out anything like that story in my head. I didn't have to do anything super bizarre, I just had to take a leap of faith.

What is a leap of faith? Think about it from the perspective of your Natural Instinct and Inner Compass. If your Natural Instinct likes to stay in the past because it uses it as evidence for what's possible for you, then a leap of faith is the complete opposite. It's following your Inner Compass to a place where nothing is certain or predictable, but doing it anyway because you know it's the right thing. It's taking that first step off the path you've been put on.

You'll find that, as you open up to your Inner Compass, you will be asked to take many leaps of faith. The Inner Compass looks toward the future, which is automatically blank, open, and unwritten. So, naturally, taking steps into the unknown will feel daunting, but I can tell you from experience that the more you do it, the better you get at it. The nervousness never goes away. Your Natural Instinct will always be there, but you surrender more quickly and move forward faster. You don't need to be transformed entirely immediately. Are you willing to just take one step into the unknown? If the answer is yes, you're ready for the next step.

Trust Your Inner Compass

Finding Your Bearings was all about using your past to understand how you may have been living by your Natural Instinct. The next step to becoming a Trailblazer is learning how to recognize your Inner Compass so you develop and strengthen it, as well as trust it to guide you in your life.

When I was little, I used to think that compasses were so magical. No matter where you turned, it would always point north. How did it know? I now understand that a compass is just a small magnetized needle that can turn in any direction. However, the magnetized needle in the compass is drawn to the Earth's magnetic field. This is why, if you turn and walk in a different direction, the needle will still point north; it's not going to follow just anything. It's attracted to that magnetic field.

The same is true for your Inner Compass. Your purposeful and fulfilling life is your north. The choices you make are either helping you walk toward that north, or taking you in a different direction. When you do things that take you away from your north, you'll feel that tug that you're out of alignment. If you look to your Inner Compass, it will point you back to the direction you want to go in. A compass is only useful if you trust and follow it—and the same goes for your Inner Compass.

CHAPTER EIGHT

THE INNER COMPASS

In the beginning of *Two Towers* by J.R.R. Tolkien, two of the main hobbits, Sam and Frodo, had just left the other members of their travel group so they could travel to Mordor to destroy the One Ring. Along this journey, they get attacked by a creature named Gollum. They end up capturing him and using him to guide them to Mordor. Frodo trusts Gollum a lot more than Sam does. As Gollum shows them the way, Sam is hesitant and doesn't feel right about where they're being led. He tries to warn Frodo that Gollum is up to something several times, but Frodo doesn't listen. He believes that Gollum will lead them on the best path. In the end, though, Gollum does lead them to a trap, and the ensuing fight with a giant spider separates Frodo and Sam from each other. When Frodo wakes up and realizes what happened, he feels regret for not listening to Sam.

Before my sickness, like Frodo, I was letting Gollum—other people's expectations/opinions and other outside influences—lead me through life. My sickness was my pause button. It is comparable to the moment Frodo woke up and realized that he'd been following the wrong person. The consequence was that I sacrificed all of myself, and I'd been doing it for so long that I no longer knew who I was or what I wanted.

Learning to Listen

Do you know who you are? If you don't, know you're not alone. This is an area of personal growth many women struggle with. They know they're unhappy, but they don't have any insight into what would make them happier. If you've been listening to your Natural Instinct for a while, your Inner Compass's voice may be very quiet. Perhaps you've never even known about your Inner Compass before, and you're getting to know it for the first time.

Once you become acquainted with your Inner Compass, it will speak to you about five areas of your life: future focus, growth, vision, inward focus, and love.

These areas build on one another; thus, improving in one will make it easier to improve in others, though you don't need to focus on them in any particular order. As you learn about these areas, notice how much the Inner Compass differs from your Natural Instinct, and how you get different results from following each one.

Future Focus

While our Natural Instinct leads us to focus on the past, our Inner Compass orients us toward the future—a blank canvas where anything is possible. Rather than using our past as evidence to limit us, our Inner Compass doesn't limit us at all, because it knows our infinite potential and evaluates us by who we can become, not by what we do or who we are right now. The beauty of future focus is that we can be whomever we want to be in the future. If our thoughts create our reality, then why would we focus on thoughts that will just continue the patterns of our past?

Following your Inner Compass will always encourage you to decide who you want to be, and to visualize yourself as that person. Thinking about yourself in this new way results in you creating something new.

Being future focused means:

- You don't limit what you can or can't do based on your past.

- You always believe that you can change. Nothing is permanent, if you don't want it to be.

- You imagine who you want to be in the future, and you think like that version of yourself, as opposed to thinking like the past version of you.

- You resist thinking on autopilot, meaning you try to be conscious and intentional about your thoughts.

- You no longer waste energy dwelling on the past and what you think it "should" have been. You now use that energy to think about and create your future.

Growth

Unlike our Natural Instinct, our Inner Compass knows that death is not the end, that just as we existed before we lived here, we will continue existing. Everything we learned before we existed here came with us, even if we don't consciously remember it. Our Inner Compass wants us to uncover these truths within us.

Have you ever heard or experienced something that was new, yet it felt familiar? Once, when I was at church, a woman shared an experience she had. I felt this really strong internal feeling that what she was saying applied to me, in a very deep and powerful way. I can't prove it to you, but somewhere within me, I just knew it was true. That was my Inner Compass, uncovering a truth that I knew subconsciously.

Just as we brought what we learned before with us, similarly, we will take all that we learn from this part of our journey with us when we pass on. Knowing this, our Inner Compass puts a high priority on growth and learning. It will always encourage us to choose growth over comfort.

Valuing Growth means:

- You look for learning and growth in all of your life experiences.

- You redefine mistakes and failure as learning opportunities, and recognize that people who make mistakes are in pursuit of growth.

- You try new things and follow your curiosities.

- You take the time to self-reflect often.

- You pursue activities that help you to learn more about yourself and uncover truths within you.

Big Vision

Having a vision is having a big picture of what you want. It's what you're working toward. Our Inner Compass desires purpose in our life, and, thus, always encourages us to create it. Unlike your Natural Instinct, your Inner Compass knows there is more to life than just survival, and will try to steer you away from merely going through the motions of life and toward being more intentional about what you do and why you do it. Your Inner Compass is focused on the long game, the journey as a whole, rather than short-term wins.

Having a Big Vision helps you:

- Have a long-term perspective and see your life as a journey.

- Not get derailed by the small setbacks; rather, you look for learning and growth in these moments, and try to see how they may help you toward your big vision.

- Make decisions with more ease, because you know where you want to go, and you choose based on whether an action can help you progress toward that or keep you from it.

- Be more intentional with your actions.

Inward Focus

Your Natural Instinct will tell you that other people have the answers you need, but your Inner Compass will tell you that all the answers you need are already within you. That's not to say you can't learn from others, but there's a difference between expecting other people to give you answers and finding answers within yourself while looking for someone to teach you how to find answers. Your Inner Compass will always lead you to have an inward focus, which means making choices based on who you want to be, as opposed to following your Natural Instinct that causes you to try to be what others want you to be so they'll like you.

Having an Inward Focus looks like:

- You look for the answers within yourself first, then you seek the help you need.

- You do things because it's who you want to be, and because you know it's right, regardless of what others' opinions are.

- You don't do things for validation, love, or acceptance. You validate yourself and love yourself first, and act from that place.

Love

While your Natural Instinct uses shame and fear, your Inner Compass always uses love. It speaks to you with grace, compassion, and understanding, and will encourage you to love yourself, as well as others. That doesn't always mean doing whatever others want you to do, but, rather, loving others no matter the circumstances. It will always encourage you to believe in your value.

Living with Love means:

- The love you feel comes from within you, not as a result of pursuing it from others.

- You work on loving yourself and seeing your value. You speak to yourself with kindness and compassion.

- You don't act out of obligation. You only do things that you can do out of love.

- You have boundaries that help you to feel love for people, no matter the circumstance.

- You can say no out of love for yourself.

Self-Reflection:

1. Now that you know how your Inner Compass speaks to you, can you think of moments where it has tried to speak to you in the past?

2. How can you better listen to your Inner Compass?

Your Life Will Change

As you start to live by your Inner Compass, you will notice changes in your life. While the specific changes will vary from person to person, four opportunities may present themselves to you. As you learn more about these opportunities, see if you can remember a time in your life that you already experienced them. You likely have. As you start to pay attention, you may find that opportunities have been presenting themselves a lot more than you previously knew. As you intentionally look for them, you'll be able to use them to develop and strengthen your ability to hear your Inner Compass.

Opportunity #1: Synchronicity

A synchronicity is when two things happen and they seem like they were planned or coordinated, but they weren't. My life has been full of these moments. Back when I had just stopped going to therapy, I felt like that part of my journey was complete, but I still felt I needed help to resolve some other struggles I was having. I didn't know what I needed, though. As I was searching, I continued to read self-help books. My friend suggested a book called *Loving What Is* by Byron Katie. I read the book and loved it, but I couldn't fully wrap my head around it. I tried to apply it in my life, but I wasn't particularly successful at it.

I had a feeling to go out to breakfast with a woman from church whom I didn't know very well. As we were talking, she brought up a podcast she'd recently started listening to and loved. I tucked the name away in my brain, but I kind of forgot about it. A week later, I was mindlessly scrolling Facebook and saw an ad featuring a woman with the headline, "How to Deal with a Difficult Family Member." After about a week of seeing this ad continue to appear, I finally asked, "Who is this woman, and why does Facebook keep showing me her face?" (This is before I really knew how Facebook ads worked.) I clicked on the ad, and I ended up buying the mini-course she was selling because it was exactly what I needed at the time. I found out she had a podcast, and I started binge-listening to all the episodes. She just seemed to speak my language, and everything she said really resonated with me.

One day, out of the blue, I made a big connection. This woman was the same person who hosted the podcast my church friend had told me about at breakfast a few weeks before. I didn't remember it until that very moment. If that wasn't enough, I was considering joining her life coaching program, so I researched her a bit more. You know what her philosophy and style of coaching are based on? Byron Katie's *Loving What Is*. The very same book that I had been trying to implement in my life for several months now. Isn't that amazing?

Let's just recap the serendipity of all of that:

1. I decide my journey with therapy is over, but still want something else to help me continue on my journey. Don't know what.

2. Friend suggests book. I read it. I love it. I try to implement it, but it's a huge paradigm shift, so I don't do it successfully.

3. I feel inspired to invite a woman to breakfast to get to know her better. She mentions a podcast that she

loves. I say, "That's cool." I don't subscribe and forget about it.

4.   A Facebook ad keeps showing me the face of a woman I don't know. I finally get fed up and click on the ad. I love the ad. I buy the thing. I become obsessed.

5.   I decide I want this woman to be my life coach. I research her background. Find out the podcast is hosted by the same woman my friend had recommended, and the program she used to become a life coach is based on the same book I'd been trying to implement.

It seems planned, but it wasn't. I could write a whole book filled with all of the synchronicities that I've seen in my life. Just within this one example, every single step I took was because I was following my Inner Compass. I had absolutely no clue that it would work out this way. However, with synchronicities, you have to notice them for them to be impactful. They're impactful because they show you that, through all of these seemingly unconnected events, your Inner Compass is leading you to what you want.

These random moments didn't seem like they were leading me to anything, but I was led to exactly what I needed to move me forward. So, while they may seem random, noticing these synchronicities will build your trust in your Inner Compass and inspire you to continue following it even when you're not sure why you're being led to do certain things.

Opportunity #2: Resistance Gets Creative

I mentioned before that whenever you want to change something or go against your Natural Instinct, resistance will appear. Maybe resistance doesn't sound like a "good" opportunity, but it actually is. First of all, if resistance has to get creative, that means you're probably following your Inner Compass and doing something that scares you.

—You go, girl.—

Second, by bringing out all this resistance, you're able to identify what resistance looks like and feels like for you. As you get really good at identifying how this shows up in your life, you can intentionally choose not to give in to it. All the energy that you save by not giving in to resistance can now be used to actually move toward your dreams.

Resistance can show up in many forms, such as wanting to eat, cleaning out your email inbox, daydreaming, writing a to-do list, scrolling social media, or having the sudden urge to clean out the millions of dishes that have piled up in your sink. It will show up differently for all of us. But as you recognize your Natural Instinct's go-to resistance techniques and choose not to engage, your Natural Instinct will start getting creative. As I was writing this book, new resistance methods came in and prevented me from writing. Sometimes it sounded reasonable. As I was sitting down to write, a thought popped into my head. "Hey. You need to fill out that form to submit to your writing coach. It needs to be done right now or it'll be late." I almost gave in. The truth was that it did need to be done, but it didn't need to be done right that second. What would have happened if I'd given in is that I would've filled out the form, and then something else would have popped up, and then something else after that. I would've done everything except for what I wanted to do, which was write.

Opportunity #3: Tests from the Universe

As you recognize areas you want to work on, you'll find many opportunities to test your commitment. I've been self-reflecting and learning how to be a better steward of my energy. I found that texting back and forth is really energy draining for me, so I wanted to have more solid boundaries for myself around that. Almost immediately after I declared this out loud, I started receiving text messages from a lot of people. I was shocked, and didn't know what to think, at first. This is what I've learned: if you say you want to work on something, the Universe is going to test you. I hope you meant it when you said you wanted to work on that thing, because you'll get a chance to prove it.

The Inner Compass wants us to grow, but it doesn't leave you hanging. Not only will it call you to more, but it will also guide you through these opportunities, if you let it. I had to decide what to do with those text messages. Was I going to reply to all of them? Ignore them? Answer a little bit? I didn't know, but I had to figure it out. With the guidance of my Inner Compass, I just took it one text message at a time. I answered a couple, at first, but didn't like that, once I engaged, it would continue into more conversation. Then I ignored some of them, but not answering didn't feel authentic to me, either. Eventually, rather than having a set protocol on how to handle text messages, I've merely taken obligation out of the equation. Just because people can get a hold of me in an instant doesn't mean I have to answer right away. Even though I will eventually respond to each text message, I do it on my own terms. I don't respond until I am energetically able to. If it will only take a few text messages, I'll just respond through text, but if it will require more than that, I try to set up a phone call. No one has turned it down or become upset about it. I know not everyone I come across will agree with my approach, and I'm OK with that. I know that I am doing what is right for me, and I can feel peace about that.

As you decide to change and follow your Inner Compass, look out for these tests from the Universe, and use your Compass to guide you through them. You may not do it perfectly, at first, but working in alignment with your Inner Compass will strengthen your connection, and ultimately your trust, and with its guidance, you'll figure it out.

Opportunity #4: Challenges for Growth

As you open yourself up to your Inner Compass and follow its guidance, you're opening yourself up to growth. It's obvious that positive opportunities help us grow, but even challenges are ultimately opportunities for growth—such as difficult relationships, the death of a loved one, getting laid off from your job, or moving to a different area. The more you follow your Inner Compass and take advantage of these chances to grow, the more opportunities you'll be presented with. What you'll find is that every opportunity your Inner Compass leads you to, even the hard ones, can be for your growth and benefit in some way. I've never regretted where my Inner Compass has led me, because I always look for how any situation helped me grow, and I can always find at least one thing to be grateful for.

Self-Reflection:

1. What synchronicities have you seen in your life? How do these moments help you build trust with your Inner Compass?

2. How is resistance showing up for you?

3. How is the Universe trying to test you? Do you have similar scenarios that keep popping up in your life? How will you address them?

4. Can you identify any opportunities for growth in your life right now?

When Sam and Frodo got separated by the big spider, Sam thought Frodo was dead. When he realized that Frodo was only stunned, he didn't run away; he went behind enemy lines and found Frodo. Our Inner Compass does the same. Even though you may have been choosing to listen to your Natural Instinct over your Inner Compass for a while, it will never abandon you. It will try to find its way back to you. If you're willing to hear it and take the opportunity to listen to it, you *will* change your life.

Now that we understand what our Inner Compass's voice sounds like and how listening to it can change our lives, how do we make sure we stay open to hearing its voice?

CHAPTER NINE

RAISE YOUR FREQUENCY

I am obsessed with music. I love playing loud music as I'm cooking, cleaning, or doing other tasks that don't require too much thinking. Back when I was a teenager, when iTunes and digital music players didn't exist, my only access to music was the radio. My first stereo had a dial to manually set the frequency of your favorite radio station. It took a lot of practice and skill to get that dial to just the right spot for the clearest signal.

Just like I had to change frequency on my stereo to hear my favorite radio station, we must also raise our frequency in order to align with our Inner Compass. To raise your frequency and get the clearest signal to your Inner Compass station, use these five tuning methods:

1. Self-Love

Self-love is placing a high value on your needs and happiness. It is loving and accepting yourself, both strengths and weaknesses, and loving the person that you are. It's treating yourself like you would treat a friend—with kindness and compassion. When you don't have self-love, you look to others for love, putting everyone else's needs before yours, and sacrificing your happiness to please them. You judge yourself by an impossible standard and criticize yourself harshly. When you're in this space, you're not going to be in tune with your Inner Compass, because you'll be too busy worrying about other people's needs and trying to get the love and belonging you crave from them.

How to have more self-love:

- Know that your value does not change based on anything you do or don't do. It's not dependent on what you achieve. You're born with inherent value. Choosing to believe this is the foundation of self-love.

- Redefine your ideal. In Chapter One, we talked about the idea of perfection that we formed in childhood. Rather than continuing to judge yourself by that impossible standard, you can accept yourself as you are—strengths and weaknesses—and let go of the idea of perfection.

- Be intentional about how you talk to yourself. Negative self-talk is the quickest way to become misaligned with your Inner Compass. Talk to yourself with kindness and compassion. Give yourself grace for the missteps. Choose encouraging words that move you forward, rather than harsh words that shame you and keep you stuck.

2. Gratitude

Gratitude is recognizing and focusing on what we have, rather than what we lack. When we choose to focus on what we lack, we are unhappy with our life. This lack of gratitude results from a scarcity mindset, where you fear that someone else getting what they want takes away from you. Thus, that fear leads to comparing your life and yourself to others, which leads to jealousy and maybe even resentment. But when you, instead, practice gratitude, you develop an abundance mindset, where you can see all that you do have in your life. You can be happy for others, and you know that, when they get what they want, it doesn't take anything from you. There's enough for everyone to have what they want.

To counteract thoughts and feelings of scarcity, incorporate gratitude practices into your life—activities that help you focus on identifying what you're grateful for. It can be something as simple as writing down what you're grateful for each morning. Gratitude is the quickest way to raise your frequency and connect with your Inner Compass, because it helps you see the abundance and beauty in the world and in your life already.

How to have more gratitude:

- Practice noticing what you're grateful for.

- Pick gratitude beliefs that you can practice throughout your day.

- When you see others getting what they want in life, use that as evidence that anything is possible, and choose to feel happy for them. See others' success as proof of what's possible for you, too.

- Any time you slip into seeing all that you lack, counteract that thought process by noticing at least five things that you have.

3. Knowing the What, Not the How

Something that can quickly knock you out of alignment with your Inner Compass is feeling a need to know *how* to get to your big vision. While it's helpful to have a goal to work toward, knowing exactly how you're going to get there is rarely helpful. The Natural Instinct will tell you that if you don't plan your path ahead of time, you'll fail. If you have perfectionist tendencies like I do, this thought can cause paralyzing fear and worry—emotions that will not align you with your Inner Compass.

Often, things will not go according to your plan. You may be tempted to assume that means something's going wrong, or you might not get to your big vision at all. But it's important to keep your focus on the end goal, the *what*. By not focusing on all the steps in between, you're saying that you trust that what you want is possible—and you trust in the journey. In this faithful energy, you can align with your Inner Compass and have the ability to know what to do next, even if it's only the first of several steps.

How to focus on the what:

- Get clear about what it is you want and choose to believe it's possible.

- Think about your big vision and then identify one step you could take to get yourself closer to it.

- Know that worry is only helpful if you can do something about it (e.g., checking if you really closed the garage door). If you can't do anything, let it go, because it's a waste of energy to worry about something you can't do anything about.

- Believe that everything will happen when it's supposed to and enjoy the journey.

- Take time to reflect on your journey thus far. By recognizing synchronicities, identifying what you've learned, and celebrating your progress, you can remember what your Inner Compass has already led you to, and regain trust in your journey.

4. Core Values

Getting clear about your core values helps you to know what is really important to you. When you're trying to live your life by these core values, you're in alignment with who you are and who you want to be, which helps you align with your Inner Compass. When you don't know your values, you're easily swayed by the values others deem as important, but you will find it hard to raise your frequency to that of your Inner Compass if you're not aligned with what *you* value.

Using your core values looks like:

- Self-reflecting and gauging whether you're living your values.

- Going through your values and thinking of ways to live them in your life now.

- Checking your choices against your values before making a decision.

5. Core Beliefs

Sometimes you know what you want in life, but no matter how many times you attempt to get it, you fail—or you don't take any action at all. This is likely because you have some limiting beliefs preventing you from changing and accomplishing what you want. Like your core values, your core beliefs were likely formed in childhood. These beliefs may be conscious or unconscious, but these thoughts, if not addressed, will continue to recreate more of your past, even if you're consciously trying to create a new future. They will keep your frequency low, and that will keep you from aligning with your Inner Compass.

Using your core beliefs looks like:

- Asking the right questions. Instead of "What's wrong with you?" you could ask, "What could be holding you back right now?" Or "How can I . . .?"

- No longer indulging in negative beliefs because you know they're not helpful and keep you stuck.

- Questioning your thoughts before assuming that they're the truth.

- Acknowledging that beliefs are not set in stone. You choose them and can change them whenever you want to.

As you continuously work on implementing these five things, you'll be able to raise your frequency and align with your Inner Compass. But being aligned is just the first part. Once you're on the same frequency, you need to turn the volume up so you can hear it.

Self-Reflection:

1. Do you feel in tune with your Inner Compass? Why or why not?

2. What activities will you start/stop doing in order to raise your frequency?

CHAPTER TEN

DAILY PRACTICES

Implementing these practices will help you turn up the volume. The good news is they don't need to take a lot of time, but they'll make a big difference as you strive to connect with and follow your Inner Compass.

A Gratitude Practice

By taking the time each day to recognize what you have, you start your day with the right focus. This mindset of abundance will have you looking for what you already have throughout the entire day and helps you to be present in your life. To practice gratitude, you'll need to find one of the many ways that best resonates with you—for example, journaling/listing what you're grateful for, a gratitude meditation, or walking around and saying what you're grateful for out loud. It may feel silly at first, but you'll get used to it quickly. Your Inner Compass is not loud, so opening your heart with gratitude helps you be the most receptive. I've gotten answers and inspiration many times while doing my gratitude practice.

Quieting the Noise

We live in a time where noise comes at us from everywhere. We hustle from one thing to the next, trying to get everything done. Most of us never have a moment of silence. Since our Inner Compass isn't loud, it's not going to yell at us or try too hard to get your attention. If you're always surrounded by noise that's louder than it is, when will you ever be able to hear it?

You need to make time in your day to sit in silence and try to hear your Inner Compass. Give it a chance to speak and be heard. I use one of two ways to do this: intentionally create silence or meditation. To intentionally create silence, turn off the music when you're driving, or sit outside on the porch by yourself. When my kids were little, I used to sit on my bathroom floor because it was the only place in my house that they wouldn't disturb me. The other method is to meditate. I used to think that meditation was this sort of woo-woo experience, but really it is just focusing on your breath and learning to control your mind, which, as you've hopefully learned so far, is a pretty important skill to have. You can try many different kinds of meditations and plenty of apps and programs, so if you don't like one, try different ones until you find one that you love.

Journaling

Journaling is a great way to get the thoughts out of your head. If you're like me, you can think a lot of thoughts really quickly. Many times, I haven't been able to hear my Inner Compass because my head was filled with too many thoughts. Dumping out all of those thoughts onto a piece of paper can be very beneficial. First, it just gets them out so your head can be clearer. Second, you might be surprised at what you're thinking. Third, I've identified limiting beliefs that I didn't know I was thinking just by journaling. Fourth, the act of having to write something down makes your brain formulate it into a sentence. If your Inner Compass is trying to make you aware of something, writing it down can help solidify those thoughts and allow you to recognize the guidance.

Consuming the Good Stuff

What are you filling your mind with? If you fill your mind with negativity, not only does it lower your frequency, but the negativity will always overpower your Inner Compass. Be conscious of who you follow on social media, the TV shows you watch, the content you read, and the music you listen to. The things you consume become thoughts in your head, and they influence the way you think and feel. If you choose to fill your mind with good things—things that inspire you, uplift you, and cause you to reflect and ponder—it will not only raise your frequency, but your Inner Compass will use other people's words and experiences to help you uncover areas of growth for yourself, and help you uncover the answers you may be seeking.

Doing Things That Energize You

We wake up each day with a certain amount of energy. We expend that energy in everything that we do, even when we think. It's like driving a car. We start with a full tank, but eventually we'll run out of gas if we don't fill up. What are you doing to fill your tank? When we don't take care of ourselves, we will default to relying on Natural Instinct because we're just trying to survive each day with whatever amount of energy we wake up with. I cannot hear my Inner Compass when I'm low on energy, so I make sure I plan activities that restore my energy throughout the day. In addition to the activities I already mentioned above, I add in hobbies, exercising, taking extra-long showers, going on walks, baking, or trying something new. What energizes me might not energize you, so you'll have to do some digging into what these activities are for you.

By no means am I saying that you need to do all of these things every day. You'll need to experiment and figure out what works best for you, but whatever you choose to do, make sure you plan it in your day. Schedule it in like an appointment, and stick to your plan. You'll have to be intentional about it, because your Natural Instinct will bring up a million other things on your to-do list and tell you that they're more important, but I promise that if you engage in even just a couple of these practices daily, you'll see a difference in your ability to align and connect with your Inner Compass.

Self-Reflection:

1. Which of these practices can you start doing now to turn up the volume on your Inner Compass?

2. When will you do them? In the morning, evening, or a mix of both?

3. How will you make sure that they happen (e.g., set a reminder, put it in your calendar, etc.)?

SECTION 4

CLEAR YOUR PATH

CHAPTER ELEVEN

THE STATE OF BEING

It was a Saturday morning. Even though my eyes were still closed, I could tell the sun was up. I tried to force myself to go back to sleep because I didn't want to get up yet, but it was no use. I was awake. I started to move around, and I could already tell it was not going to be a good day. I felt cranky, annoyed, and defeated.

Three years ago, we made an out-there decision to go for a new job position at my husband's company. It was rotational, meaning that he would work in Africa for twenty-eight days and then be off for twenty-eight days. It was a job position we've known about his whole career but never wanted to do. But then we started creating this vision of what we wanted our life to be, which included moving somewhere new, and this unconventional job not only fit into that vision, but it felt like the right thing to do. We applied for it, but there were limited positions, so we had to wait for a space to open up. Once it did, we were given the runaround for a bit. After a lot of work on my husband's part, they told us we'd be given an official offer within two weeks.

The end of those two weeks was the day before this particular Saturday morning, and we still didn't have an offer, so I woke up feeling all sorts of negative things. As I lay in bed, my husband came in and I cried to him about it. He tried to console me, but it didn't help. I wanted to be mad. I felt justified in it, so I continued to sulk in my bed and indulge in negative thoughts. I was basically throwing a tantrum because I wasn't getting what I wanted. I eventually got out of bed and went downstairs—not because I wanted to, but simply out of obligation to my family. I sort of just moped around the house, taking care of things here or there, but not fully engaged in anything. I had done enough work on myself to know that I was operating from my Natural Instincts. I knew my thoughts were creating my suffering. I just didn't care because I wanted to be mad.

By the afternoon, I was tired of feeling negative and wanted to feel differently. Knowing that I was the cause of my own suffering, I started to turn my mood around. I had received a mug in the mail that I'd ordered a few weeks before and forgotten about, so I chose to let myself feel excited and grateful for it. I paid attention to the thoughts I was thinking. I let go of the negative thoughts that weren't helping, and I asked myself a pivotal question: "What can I do right now?"

I didn't know when we would get the official offer. I didn't know when I was going to be moving. But I did know that both would happen. Knowing that, I imagined I was in the process of moving already and focused on something that needed to be done that I could do now: packing up the basement. Since I would have to pack that area eventually, why not pack it now?

I grabbed boxes, tape, and a Sharpie, and went downstairs. I blasted some music, and I started packing. An hour or so later, I emerged from that basement with a different outlook and attitude. I knew that everything would work out in the best timing. Best of all, rather than worrying about the future, I pulled myself back into the present, where I could be with my family and feel happy in my current circumstance.

The third step in the Trailblazer process, Clear Your Path, is all about taking action. While Finding Your Bearings and Following Your Inner Compass are mostly inner work, Clearing Your Path is taking all of that inner work and putting it into action. Understanding ourselves and what we want is essential and feels great, but if we don't actually do anything different, nothing changes.

Simply taking action is not enough, because not all action is created equal. It's taking the *right* actions that will propel you forward on your path. How do you know what the right action is? That's the million-dollar question. A great process that I love is the Be-Do-Have model. This model has been around for a while, but I love the simplicity of it. The HAVE represents what you want, which for this book is a fulfilling and purposeful life. The DO is what you have to do to get what you want. The BE is who you need to be in order to get what you want. So, basically, if you *be* the person who already has what you want, you will *do* what needs to be done to get what you want to *have*. Be-Do-Have. Makes sense, right?

The problem is that most of us don't live in this way. We switch up the order of the words to Have-Do-Be. But this doesn't end up working in the long run, as we don't get what we want. See if any of these examples resonate with you:

- **Have-Do-Be:** You wait to have more of something (time, money, fewer kids at home, opportunities, etc.) before you take action and do what you need to do to be what you want to be. Example: When I *have* more time, I'll be able to *do* more things that I love, and then I'll *be* happy. This model doesn't work because you'll never have enough of whatever you think you need to get started, which means you never do anything.

- **Do-Be-Have:** You think that if you *do* more, then you'll *be* something and then *have* what you want. For example, if you keep the house clean, cook homemade meals every day, and get all the laundry done, then you'll be a good mom, and then you'll have a happy family. But that doesn't work. If you think you have to do all of those things to be a good mom, you'll be overwhelmed and stressed. Will you really have a happy family if you're always overwhelmed and stressed?

- **Do-Have-Be:** You think that if you *do* more, then you'll *have* more, and then you'll *be* whatever it is you want. Example: If I work harder, I'll have more money, and then I'll be happy. This doesn't work, because, if you have to work hard all the time, will you have any time left to use that money and enjoy your life?

You can see how the word order matters here, and there's only one way to do it. You have to BE first. When I woke up on that Saturday morning, upset about not having that job offer, I was operating in a Have-Be-Do model. I wanted to have the job offer so I could be certain about our new life path, so I could start packing. The truth was that we had a lot to do, and everything was going to move very fast once my husband got the official job offer, so the more we could get done beforehand, the better. But I hadn't taken any action because I didn't know when we'd move, and I couldn't pack things too early because we needed to use them. Once I decided to think like the future me who had already gotten the official job offer, I was able to find something that I could do immediately. Two weeks after that day, we got the job offer, and I'm so grateful I had gotten started rather than waiting.

CHAPTER TWELVE

YOUR FUTURE SELF

I'm a dreamer. I love to dream of the future and what's possible. I love brainstorming and coming up with new ideas. But with all of that dreaming, I struggled, in the beginning, to make my dreams a reality. I used to make that mean that it wasn't possible for my dreams to come true, but I now know that's not accurate.

My dreams have always been possible, I just didn't know how to make them happen. The biggest game changer in my life has been learning how to take the right actions that get me to where I want to go. That is done by first identifying who my future self (the version of me that already has what I want) is and choosing to be that person now.

Thinking into the future can be hard because it hasn't happened yet. When you think about your future from the viewpoint of your Natural Instinct, you use the information from your past. While from that place, the future is easier to think about because you have something to base it off of; you don't want to create more of your past. Thus, you have to look from the viewpoint of your Inner Compass, which is based on a future that can only be created by your imagination. It takes more energy to think about the future in this way, so if you are struggling, I just want you to know that's completely normal, and it will get easier to do with time and practice.

You can use three steps to help imagine your future self. As you go through each one, keep an open mind, align with your Inner Compass, and write down the thoughts and ideas that come to mind. Don't feel like you have to get this perfect the first time. You can always add and tweak things as your desires or circumstances change. Sometimes it helps to go through the process once, walk away, and then come back to it again. The clearer you can get on this part, the better. Remember, this is what helps you know the difference between just taking action and taking the right action, so take your time.

1. Let go of the past

This first step is more about making a choice to let go of the past, because, if you base your future on your past, you will use evidence from the past to support and hold on to limiting beliefs; thus, you'll only create more of your past.. Have you ever thought of something you wanted to do, but then you talked yourself out of it because of a situation from your past? As a homeschool mom, whenever other moms find out I homeschool, many comment on how they think it's great and how they admire me—and then they say how they could never do it. Most of the time they say they can't because they don't have the patience. But who's to say that they can't develop patience? Their past says they can't.

Their past shows them that they've already yelled at their kids too many times, and shows them all the frustrating afternoons at the kitchen table doing hours of homework. It points to those things and then says that homeschooling will not look any different than that. When those moms think they can't homeschool and use their past to prove that, it's no surprise that they doubt their ability.

The reason it's important to let go of this cycle is you'll never dream bigger than your past if you don't. As soon as you try to dream bigger than your past, your Natural Instinct will use your limiting beliefs and past to bring you back down to what's "realistic." So, in the end, all that's left for you to dream is what you've already accomplished in your past. Hence, you recreate your past. Our past can be a great place to learn from, but it's not a great place to create from.

Before I decided to homeschool, I had to let go of my past, as well. I never had considered myself a patient person, and a lot of past experiences showed that I wouldn't be successful. But I trusted in my Inner Compass, which was the part of me that actually brought up homeschooling as an option in the first place. I moved forward, trusting that I could be better than I had been in the past, and that I could create something new. As you start to create your future self, notice whether you're trying to find proof from your past to invalidate its possibility. If you are:

Choose to let the past go, and remember that to create something new, you have to think something new.

Remember that beliefs are a choice, and that it's just as possible for you to change as it is for you to stay the same.

2. Get clear on what you want

Once you stop using your past to gauge what's possible for you, the future starts opening up, and you start seeing the endless possibilities available to you. Once I stopped using my past as a barometer of what was possible for me, I started dreaming bigger. When I became a huge fan of the British TV show "Doctor Who," I felt this strong pull toward England. My husband felt it, too, and after much discussion, we decided we wanted to move there. We didn't know when or how, but it was our big dream. At the time, my husband's company had an office in London, so he tried to get that position. After some time of trying, it became clear to us that it wasn't going to work out. I was devastated at first because it felt like my dream wasn't going to happen. With time, though, I saw this as a blessing.

If we'd gotten that position, we would've had to live in a suburb or near the city. I don't like the city. We wanted to live in the countryside. Another main reason we wanted to live in

England was to have easy access to the rest of Europe so we could explore new places. But we wouldn't really have that much time to do that, since my husband would've been working a normal nine-to-five with the same limited vacation time he had then. This position that I was sad about not getting wasn't really going to give me the life I wanted. It would have gotten me to England in the easiest way possible, which sounded great, but it wouldn't have provided the lifestyle I wanted to go along with it.

From this experience, I learned that you have to get as clear as possible about what it is you want. I did this by envisioning that dream life in my mind. What did I really want? Nothing was too silly or too unrealistic. I just allowed myself to say what I truly wanted, without ridicule. I envisioned rolling English countryside landscapes and quiet evenings of watching the sunset. I envisioned not being held down to any school or work schedule, and having the ability to travel and explore other countries with my husband and kids whenever we wanted. Our source of income would allow us to live and work from anywhere, and would allow us time off and flexibility. When I envisioned my dream life, it felt adventurous, free, tranquil, and easy. The clearer I could get about what I wanted, the easier it became to see my future self.

Do this for your dream life. Sit down, close your eyes, and imagine what this dream life looks like for you. Don't hold back, don't put any limitations on it. Visualize it and then write it down. Think about the big goals you have, but also think about your relationships and your lifestyle. How do you want to feel in your life? What is the vibe? The clearer you get on this, the easier the next step will be, so take the time to do this a few times, if you need to.

3. Imagine if you had what you want already

Now that you're clear about what you really want, you can now identify your future self, so you can start being that person. Imagine that the future version of you has the life you wrote down in Step Two. What does your future self do? Does she have certain routines or habits? How does she think? What does she think about and what does she not think about? How does she feel?

When I envision my future self, she's unconventional and thinks outside of the box. She trusts her Inner Compass to guide her and is confident in her ability to recognize it, even when no one else believes her. She allows herself to dream, but also takes action. She knows her value, so she doesn't worry about what others think of her or how much of her to-do list she gets done in a day. She values experiences and growth, so she spends money on things that help her achieve those two things. She knows when she takes care of herself, she can better take care of others, so she has a morning routine and makes time for things that she enjoys and that energize her. She spends quality time with her husband and children. It's important for her to be a good steward of her energy, so she's cautious about what she allows into her life, whether it's information, media, or people.

If you're not used to thinking about your future self, this can be hard to do. That's why I wanted to give you a glimpse into my future self, but I don't want you to compare your future self to mine. They won't look exactly the same, which is good, because they're not supposed to.

If you're struggling in answering these questions for yourself, here are a few suggestions to help you:

- Try doing an activity to help you align with your Inner Compass before trying again (go back to Chapter Eight for ideas).

- Did you come up with core values or core beliefs from Section Two that could help you here?

- Try doing a meditation where you imagine meeting your future self face-to-face. What would she say to you? What does she look like? What advice does she give you?

Self-Reflection:

1. Compare your future self with what you're doing right now. What's missing? What could you improve?

131

CHAPTER THIRTEEN

CLOSING THE GAP

Now that you can see who you need to be, you can start focusing on what you need to do.

You likely have a gap between who you are now and who you want to be, so you will need to take action and make changes to close that gap. This chapter is where all of that action and work takes place. This is the first time that I've really delved into the topic of taking external action. There's a reason for that. We're told that in order to change our life, we need to take action. While that's technically true, as we've learned, not all action takes you to where you want to go.

We need to take the right action. There's a quote that defines insanity as doing the same things again and again while expecting different results. This is what we're doing when we listen to our Natural Instincts. Therefore, it is important to first do the internal work so you can determine the right action when the time comes to take external action.

Before therapy, I was trying to work on the anger I felt. I tried different external actions, but I always got the same results— because I wasn't changing anything *internally*. Changing actions may feel like we're trying something different, but, in reality, we're thinking the same thoughts, and, therefore, creating the same result. I don't know about you, but when I was doing that over and over in my life, insanity is exactly what I felt. I didn't understand how I could try all of these different actions, yet get the same results. We can't just change our actions if we want different results; we need to change the voice we're listening to, and we need to be a different person on the inside. As we try to be that person, we will be led to the right actions that will take us where we want to go.

What changes do you need to make in order to be your future self? While the specific changes vary from person to person, all Trailblazers need to address five categories in some way:

1. Thoughts

2. Decision-making

3. Environment

4. Habits

5. Relationships

1. Thoughts

As you're making changes, start with your thoughts. You've done a lot of this inner work while Finding Your Bearings, but that's only half the battle. As you identify and let go of your limiting beliefs, what beliefs can you replace them with? You need to take action and start thinking thoughts that will help you get to where you want to go. One simple example from my life has to do with my house. I used to be very particular about keeping it clean. I was constantly picking up my kids' toys, and would often get frustrated when the living room was cluttered with their stuff. I had a rule that the majority of their toys had to stay in their room.

As I started doing my inner work, I realized that my future self valued quality time with her kids over a clean house. In the past, I didn't get to fully enjoy my kids because I was too busy picking up their toys or feeling overwhelmed and frustrated. I knew that if I didn't want to be frustrated by the mess, I would need to change how I saw the mess; thus, I needed to start with my thoughts. So when I would walk into the living room and see all of their mess, rather than think about how messy it was, I would think, "My family really lived it up today." It sounds ridiculous, but it did wonders for my mindset. Rather than seeing a mess, I would see their imaginative Lego creations and the books they had enjoyed reading. I started seeing the "mess" as proof that my kids were still living with me in my house. They'll grow up one day and my living room will be clean all the time, so by changing my mindset I was able to start feeling gratitude when I saw that mess. As you walk down your path and identify the things you want to change, you also need to identify thoughts you need to change to get that different result.

Action Steps:

1. Evaluate your thoughts and beliefs and write them down.

2. Identify the results that those thoughts and beliefs are creating in your life. If you're not getting the results you want, identify a new, more helpful thought that can guide you to what you want.

2. Decision-Making

How many times have you said to yourself that you're going to do something, but then you never actually do it? Yeah, me too. In fact, I found that I did that a lot. I've filled notebooks full of ideas and projects that have never happened. I've written out my whole business plan, just to change it all the next week. I've said that I want to lose twenty pounds and then bought a large McDonald's french fry. What I've come to learn is that you know you've made a decision only if you're taking action. If you're not doing anything, you haven't really decided. It can be hard to recognize that you're not making decisions because your rationalizations for not taking action are really convincing, and sometimes they may even be true. What's not true is that you have to wait for those things in order to take steps toward your goal. Maybe you need $15,000 and you don't actually have the money in your account. But are you really not able to do anything? Could you get a second job, get takeout less, or create a budget and stick to it? If you have truly decided to do something, you will figure out a next step. If haven't decided you should ask yourself why. Are you scared of making the wrong decision, so you keep looking for the perfect solution? Do you feel self-doubt, so you keep changing your mind rather than committing? You can't be a Trailblazer if you are not making decisions and taking action. The better you get at identifying when you're not taking action, and getting clear as to why, the easier and faster it becomes to Clear Your Path.

Action Steps:

1. Write down the goals you are trying to achieve and identify how you've decided to accomplish them.

2. Think about each of those decisions and ask, "What is one step that I can take right now to get closer to my goal?"

3. Plan when you're going to do it and put it into your calendar.

3. Environment

While you don't have to travel to somewhere exotic or challenge yourself to your limits, there's a reason that most self-discovery books like *Eat, Pray, Love* and *Wild* take place in far-off, exotic places or include extreme, challenging situations. When we find ourselves in an unfulfilling life, where we're constantly recycling our past thoughts, thus creating more of our past, we find our external world matches that pattern. We have routines and habits that we get stuck in repeating.

It can be hard to do work on changing your thoughts when your external environment is exactly the same because your external environment reminds you of your old way of thinking. This can cause you to relapse into your old thoughts again. Changing your environment in some way can help you to live as your future self. I'm not saying you have to go somewhere exotic or climb a mountain, but perhaps you can declutter or rearrange the furniture. Maybe you can designate a particular space for your morning reflection or meditation. If your space is kind of dark and your future self would love light, put up more mirrors, open the blinds more, or get more lamps.

My future self values experiences over stuff, so I changed up my home decor to reflect that. I was no longer interested in a perfectly decorated Instagram-worthy home. I wanted a home that reminded me of the memories we've made. I added souvenirs from our travels, pictures of our favorite places, a map where we can put a pin in everywhere we've been, and words and sayings on the wall that give off the adventure vibe. We began to really love our home. It reminds us of what we value, and anytime we pass something on our wall or on the shelves, we're reminded of all of our adventures. It feels like the home of someone who's adventurous, and it inspires me to keep being adventurous, not only in my travels but also as I make changes in myself.

Action Steps:

1. Write down everything about your environment. What is your daily routine from when you get up to when you go to sleep? What is your home environment like? Your work environment?

2. Go through and list the parts of your environment that do not align with the life you are trying to create.

3. Identify what needs to change and what actions you can take now to change it.

4. Habits

Thinking about your future self, do you have any habits you might need to stop or start in order to be that version of you? Does your future self stay up late? How often does she scroll social media? Does she have a morning and/or nightly routine? Do the habits that you have move you toward being your future self or hold you back?

In the beginning of my marriage, we got Dish TV. Neither I nor my husband grew up with this luxury, so we were so excited to have so many shows at our disposal. After my sickness, as we were re-evaluating our life, we realized that we spent a lot of time watching TV shows. With the invention of DVR, you never had to decide which shows to watch because you could record them and watch them all. We were wasting our lives away in front of that TV. We decided to cancel it. Without the easy distraction of TV, we had more free time on our hands and found new activities that brought us more fulfillment and happiness.

Are you being intentional about what you spend your time on? I added a morning routine habit. As an entrepreneur, wife, and mother, I need a lot of energy to show up as my best self. In the past, I would just wing it every morning, not really having any solid routine. Some days were OK, and other days were not great at all. After identifying the habits of my future self, I knew she had some sort of morning routine. I've read a lot of books and blog articles about these routines and I'd tried to be consistent in the past, but I hadn't been successful. But now that I knew my future self, I combined that image with the knowledge I had and curated a morning routine that looked different from any other I'd tried before. I made sure to only include the activities that brought me the most energy and that I would do consistently. Now, I start my day with more energy and experience good mornings a majority of the time. My interactions with my family have changed for the better, and they even see a difference in my overall mood and energy level.

Action Steps:

1. Write down your habits and the activities that take up your time each day.

2. Determine whether your current habits and activities are helping you create the life you want, and decide whether you will keep them or let them go.

3. List habits and activities that you want to start, and make a plan on how you will start incorporating them.

5. Relationships (Setting Boundaries)

Sometimes certain relationships in our life make it harder for us to be our future self. In these cases, you may need to set boundaries. Boundaries are a delineation of what is and is not OK. I see boundaries as guidelines that make it possible for you to show up with love and as your best self in any situation. Boundaries are not used as punishment, nor are they a way to manipulate others to do what you want them to do. In fact, boundaries are not actions that other people have to take ("If you yell at me, you'll have to leave"), but what you will do ("If you yell at me, I'll leave the room"). Boundaries make it possible for you to meet your needs so you can show up genuinely and compassionately for those around you. Setting boundaries also helps you determine when to say no. Women often want to help others, so they will often say yes to things, even if they really don't want to do them. We think it's the nice thing to do, but if you're only doing it out of obligation, it will turn to bitterness and resentment. Brené Brown says, "Daring to set boundaries is about having the courage to love ourselves, even when we risk disappointing others."

Action Steps:

1. List out your boundaries. What are you OK with and not OK with?

2. Determine whether any of the relationships in your life are holding you back from being who you want to be. What would allow you to show up as your most loving and compassionate self in these relationships?

3. Start living those boundaries now. Say no, leave, or express your boundaries if you need to, but commit to upholding your boundaries with others so you can be who you want to be.

CHAPTER FOURTEEN

OBSTACLES

As you start making changes and Clearing Your Path, you'll run into obstacles. They're all part of the journey, and no one is exempt from them. Many obstacles may come up, but there are four specific ones that I see commonly:

1. Information overload

2. Fear of failure

3. Reactions of others

4. Standing alone

These obstacles are sneaky. When they show up in the beginning, they sound reasonable, so you don't see that they eventually limit you. I've been guilty of letting every single one of these obstacles hold me back at some point in my life. Becoming aware of them and knowing how they show up stops me from being blindsided by them, and allows me to keep Clearing My Path.

1. Information Overload

Oftentimes, as you're Clearing Your Path, you're forced to learn new skills and ways of being to get to where you want to be. You can find a lot of resources out there in the form of books, podcasts, gurus/mentors, blogs, Facebook groups, and online courses. While it's amazing to live in a day and age where we have all this information at our fingertips, it can also set us back.

Passive Action

Sometimes gathering information seems like taking action, but, in reality, you're not actually doing anything to move forward on your path. When you read a book, do you just move on to another book when you're done, or do you actually try to apply what you learned in some way? You have to be careful that you're not using learning as a distraction from taking action.

Too Much Information

Too much information can overwhelm your mind and can prevent you from making a decision at all. The perfect example of this is when I go to The Cheesecake Factory. That menu has, like, five million options. That's a slight exaggeration, but I can get overwhelmed by that menu. I'm always the last one to order, and, up until the millisecond before the server gets to me, I'm still going back and forth and freaking out about my choice. Too much information is not always the best thing.

Looking for All the Answers

There's nothing wrong with consuming information, but it becomes a setback when you're wanting that information to give you all the answers. This can look like searching for the perfect guru/mentor to give you the step-by-step guide; buying endless online courses and low-price offers from Facebook ads; asking people in Facebook groups what you should do; and mindlessly consuming podcasts, blogs, or whatever you can fit in. This becomes an obstacle because the answers that you need aren't out there, they're *within you*. When you focus on finding the answers in these outside sources, you will never find them, because there is no perfect program or perfect answer from anyone else but yourself. In addition, when you are constantly consuming information, do you leave time to quiet your mind and listen to the place that will actually lead you to the right answers—your Inner Compass?

This doesn't mean that you can't get helpful information from others, or that you shouldn't seek it out. You will undoubtedly need to tap into others' expertise to learn, but it will only help you if you're mindfully consuming information. Thus, as you're looking for help, you should seek someone to help you learn a specific thing, rather than to give you all the answers. Understand that this person isn't going to know what's best for you, but that they can still help you learn something. I call these crossroad moments. We're all individuals on our own life journey, but sometimes our path crosses with another person. Either we learn something from them, they learn something from us, or we both learn from each other.

Self-Reflection:

1. How does your future self consume information? Is she constantly consuming? How does she know when she's consuming too much?

2. Write down all your sources of information. This could include podcasts, websites, music playlists, TV shows/movies, and books. Go through each one and consider these three questions:

> a. Why are you watching/listening/reading this? What do you think you will get from it?
>
> b. Is this preventing you from being your future self? Is it preventing you from taking action?
>
> c. Are you applying what you're learning from this resource, or is it just a distraction?

2. Fear of Failure

While I dedicated a whole chapter to fear, I wanted to address this specific fear because it may come up a lot when you're Clearing Your Path. The biggest problem with this fear is that you often don't recognize that you're struggling with it. Fear rarely shows up as fear, but is often disguised as something reasonable.

The Disguises of Fear

In the process of writing this book, fear has come up about a million times, but not once did I think, "I'm scared of failure right now." It showed up as sudden urges to jump on social media, wanting to play music (even though I know music with lyrics causes me to write more slowly), needing a snack, daydreaming, and random thoughts of things that I need to get done around the house. In the end, none of these things sound bad, right? They're innocent-enough activities, but I knew that

147

they were just different manifestations of fear showing up. Writing this book is scary. I'm doing something new and putting my thoughts and experiences out into the world for everyone to critique. My Natural Instinct is trying to keep me from doing it.

As you're Clearing Your Path, you'll be doing new things. You'll be thinking differently and forming new habits, and it will freak your Natural Instinct out a bit. Knowing that all of the newness might trigger this fear of failure, look at the actions you're taking, especially the seemingly harmless ones. Are they distracting you from the action you want to be taking? If you start paying attention to the cues, you'll likely see patterns emerge, and you'll get really good at noticing when you're feeling that fear of failure.

Defining Failure

What is failure, anyway? Is it not doing something perfectly the first time? Is it making more than ten mistakes? Failure is relative and will be defined differently with each person. So, if you get to define failure, why not define it as giving up? You only fail if you give up, and everything else can just be considered learning. What if you looked at failure as a good thing? It makes me think of the movie *The Incredibles*. The bad guy creates this robot machine that repairs itself, and every time someone defeats it, it learns from that, and then can't be defeated in the same way again. What if that's how we looked at our mistakes? Every time we make one, we learn from it and become stronger as a result.

When I know that I'm fearing failure, I call my Natural Instinct out. I'll say or think, "No. I don't need to do that right now. We're doing this, instead. You're just feeling fear of failure right now, and failure would be giving up, which I'm not going to do." Calling out your Natural Instinct will help you intentionally choose not to let fear hold you back from what you want and keep you moving forward on your path.

Self- Reflection:

1. How would your future self handle fear of failure? How would she define failure, and what does this definition do for her?

2. Write down any recent "failures" that you've had. Redefine them from the perspective of your future self.

3. Reactions of Others

As you go about making changes in your life, not everyone will be supportive. Some people may get angry. This can be really hard when it's someone within your family or someone you really love. Something to ask yourself is whether keeping the people in your life happy will take you to the life you want to live. When I was Finding My Bearings, I realized that so much of my unhappiness was based on spending so much of my time and energy trying to make other people happy. When the choices I made were dependent on how other people would react, they only benefited the other people (and they were not even happy 100 percent of the time), and those choices led to a very unhappy and unfulfilling life for me. That's not the life I wanted to live, and I'm guessing that's not the life you want, either.

When we become afraid of negative reactions, it can cause us to stop in our tracks because we're scared of losing people. I'm not going to say that it's easy, but what I do want to offer is that, by doing what you know to be right for yourself and allowing people to feel however they want to, you can feel peace no matter the outcome of the situation. When it comes to how others react, I have some thoughts for you to consider as you navigate Clearing Your Path. Each relationship will be different, and it's not always predictable, but as you stay open, curious, and continue showing up as the person you want to be, then the next step will present itself.

You Never Had Control

When someone stops clearing their path because of others' reactions, they believe they can control other people's emotions.

People-pleasers have this belief. They get really good at predicting and doing whatever the other wants them to do so the other person can be happy and love them. When they succeed, they believe that what they *did* got them the love they wanted. An example is trying to make your kid happy. When they're happy, we tell ourselves, "I'm good at making my kid happy." So we feel good. But the times we're not successful, we tell ourselves, "I'm not able to make my kid happy," which quickly spirals to other thoughts like, "I'm a horrible mom," or "I don't know what I'm doing."

But the thing is that, in both scenarios, you never had control. Your child is the one who gets to decide if they want to be happy or not. Sometimes that works in your favor, sometimes it doesn't. Either way, though, you don't get to take credit for it. This is true for any of our relationships. When you understand that the only thing within your control is how you show up in the world, you will feel free to continue Clearing Your Path.

They Just Need Time

When you're in a relationship for a while, you form a dynamic. As you start to change yourself, the dynamics in your different relationships will change, as well. Change is hard for most people, so this will throw people off. For example, my husband and I had a fight one day, but since I'd been learning how to control my own thoughts and emotions, rather than fighting back like I'd always done in the past, I said I wanted to be alone and think about it for a little bit. That really annoyed him, which I was so confused about. Did he really prefer that I stay and yell at him instead? He didn't want that, but he was also confused by my new reaction. After talking it out more, we resolved our issue. Since then, the way we argue has shifted tremendously, but it took that initial shock and time to get there, as we had to continue working on ourselves and shift to our new dynamic. Some people in your life will want to understand and will eventually be your greatest supporters, but the initial shock can be hard. Through time, you can help them shift to the new dynamic, and your relationship will be stronger for it. The best thing you can do for these people is continue to be who you want to be, uphold your boundaries, and allow them to come around on their own time.

The Natural Separation

When people are angry at us, we tend to believe their emotion means we did something wrong, that we caused it. You know by now that isn't true. If we create our emotions by our thoughts, then that means other people create their emotions by their thoughts. When others react to our choices, they're reacting to their perception of our choices. Depending on the person, they may see your changes and feel inspired to make changes of their own, or they might disagree and remove themselves from your life.

This is why I don't believe that you need to cut anyone out of your life, most of the time. If you're showing up each day, being the person you want to be, the people who don't align with that will naturally remove themselves. The things you value aren't the things that they value and they are not going to *want* to stay.

I've had this happen multiple times in my life. I had a really good friend of many years. We had our well-established dynamic, but as I started to change and grow, I noticed some things I wasn't happy with. I started acting differently and making choices aligned with what I thought was right, and she slowly started retreating. I wanted to keep this friendship, and I tried to do so, but she eventually stopped responding altogether. At first, I felt really angry and hurt about this, like I was the one being rejected, but now I see differently.

Clearly, she didn't want the new dynamic—she wanted things to stay the same, while I didn't. In order for both of us to be happy, we naturally had to go our separate ways. This is the perfect example of a crossroad moment. It wasn't easy to let this friendship go. While it had brought me a lot of happiness before, I understood why it ended, and that, perhaps, it was the best thing for me—and maybe even her. Now I can look back on the good times of our friendship with fondness, gratitude, and hope for her continued happiness. When we allow others the same courtesy of thinking and being who they want to be, we can feel love for them regardless of whether they decide to stay in our life or decide to walk away. That kind of peace, in addition to the joy we feel from living the life that we want, is priceless.

4. Standing alone

Let's review what we said at the beginning about Natural Instinct. Back in the early days of our ancestors, belonging to the pack was part of survival, so our Natural Instinct still believes that. It tells us that belonging and fitting in is necessary for survival. That's not really true, at least not in the same way anymore, but it explains our desire for love and belonging. This was one of my biggest fears as I was clearing my own path. What I learned is that your thoughts about being alone scare you more than the act of actually being alone. As an example, in the beginning of my journey, I tried to hold on to the relationships that I had because I was scared of losing them. I reasoned that if I lost them, what would I have left?

Having nothing seemed lonely, empty, and sad. However, when you focus on what you have to lose, it will be harder to continue Clearing Your Path. There's no escaping the fact that being a Trailblazer means you have to walk the path alone. It's your own personal journey; no one else can do it for you. But it doesn't mean you're the only person out there doing it. In her book *Braving the Wilderness*, Brené Brown quotes one of her friends, Jen Hatmaker, who said something that has always stuck out to me: "Put one foot in front of the other enough times, stay the course long enough to actually tunnel into the wilderness, and you'll be shocked how many people already live out there—thriving, dancing, creating, celebrating, belonging. It is not a barren wasteland. It is not unprotected territory. It is not void of human flourishing. The wilderness is where all the creatives and prophets and system-buckers and risk-takers have always lived, and it is stunningly vibrant. The walk out there is hard, but the authenticity out there is life."

By Clearing Your Path and moving forward, some people may walk away, and it may feel scary to be standing alone, but you'll soon find you're not the only one out there. Many other women are out there being Trailblazers in their own lives. They're each on their own path alone, as well, but by seeing each other, you'll all feel less alone. By letting go of the relationships that aren't aligned with who you want to be, you'll have more energy to focus on the relationships that remain and form new relationships that, from the beginning, will already be healthier than the ones you had to give up.

Self-Reflection:

1. Are there any relationships in your life that need to change in order to align with the life you are trying to create?

2. Are you afraid of being alone? Are you holding on to any of your relationships because you are afraid of being alone?

3. Write out all of the prominent relationships in your life. Consider these questions as you think about each one:

   a. Can you be your authentic self in this relationship? Why or why not?

   b. Does this relationship help you move toward the life you're trying to create? Why or why not?

   c. What would you like to change in this relationship?

   d. What can you do to help this relationship improve?

LIVING A DARING LIFE

CHAPTER FIFTEEN

MY DARING LIFE

I was driving down the road on the way home from picking up food for dinner. No stoplights. Only one or two other cars on the road. Trees lining both sides. The windows were down, and I could feel the cool breeze.

That's when it hit me hard.

A feeling of overwhelming gratitude. I cannot fully put into words how much I love the life I live. It's so different from where I started. All of the steps, both big and small, all of the changes I've made in myself have led to this moment. Where my life used to be filled with so much anger and negativity, it's now filled with love, positivity, and levity. I'm able to enjoy and soak up every second I have with my kids. I'll be sad when they grow up and move on, but I feel peace knowing I made the most of the time I had with them. My relationship with my husband went through the wringer, and I wasn't sure we were going to make it, at a couple points, but now it's better than I knew it could be. For the first time in a long time, I can see how England might be possible for us, but the funny part is that I don't really know if I need to live there anymore. The Pacific Northwest has a lot of what England had to offer me, though I wouldn't count it out yet—I still long for that English countryside.

The best part of my life is not anything physical, but what I feel. *Freedom.*

I feel free to want what I want.

I feel free to make time for what matters to me.

I feel free of others' expectations.

I feel free to be me.

What Was Missing

When I started my journey, I wasn't really sure what I wanted, because I wasn't really sure what was missing. Looking back, I now see *I* was missing. So much of what I'd based my life on was not coming from me. I had molded myself to fit the expectations of those around me because I hadn't learned how to love myself, making it impossible for me to break free from those expectations, no matter how much I tried. While I was doing a lot for those around me, I was suppressing the *best* parts of me. The parts of me that I had been conditioned to believe were my weaknesses, but, in reality, were my greatest strengths.

When I permitted myself to be my full self, I could step into my power for the first time and be who I always knew I had the potential to be.

As women, we're told—often by each other—that focusing on ourselves is selfish, but when you focus on yourself and who you want to be, you can show up so much better for those you love. I know this because I live this. I remember the woman I used to be, and I know the woman I am now. There is no comparison.

I'm a very different person, for the better, and I realize now how selfish it was of me to withhold the best parts of myself from my family all in the name of self-sacrifice. My husband and kids have had to make changes and sacrifices, too. They have to sacrifice some time with me because I take time for myself, and I run a business. They have to help me more, whether it's cleaning, eating cereal for dinner once a week (which they love, by the way), or entertaining themselves every once in a while. But if you asked them, they wouldn't want to go back to our life before. Because now they get a mom who barely ever yells, who listens to them more, who lets them keep their toys all over the living room floor, and who is really present when she's with them. They get the best version of their mom.

I Am a Trailblazer

The beauty of being a Trailblazer is that the life you end up creating is better than the life that you had planned. Yes, it's been hard, and at times I didn't know how I would keep going, but I never gave up—and now here I am, in my beautiful, daring life that's been worth every single step.

Being a Trailblazer never ends. Everything I wrote in this book, I still apply and live in my life today. Sometimes I give in to my Natural Instinct, though not as much as I used to. Sometimes I avoid my Inner Compass, though I get to surrender a lot faster. I'm always Clearing My Path in some way, and I don't think that ever ends for any of us. And while I have done a lot of work in Finding My Bearings, I still have limiting beliefs that come up and try to derail me (and sometimes they do), but I become aware of them a lot more quickly, and they don't keep me stuck for nearly as long. Being a Trailblazer is not a one-time deal. It's a lifelong process that I'm committed to living every day. Some days I do it better than others, and some days are harder than others, but regardless, I show up each day, giving it my all.

Nothing I've accomplished in my life is out of reach for anyone. In fact, I wrote this book because I believe the joy I've found in my life is possible for you, and I want you to have it!

CHAPTER SIXTEEN

YOUR DARING LIFE

Not everyone chooses to be a Trailblazer. Even when they see that they could have the life they want, they still choose to stay on the path they've been put on. It's not easy to take that leap of faith, but for those who are willing to take it, the reward is great. Imagine a life that has more of you in it. I don't just mean more of you, in the physical sense, but more of who you are. A life where you are doing the things you love with the people you love the most. It's a life where your dreams are not limited, and you go after what you want because you know it's possible. You wake up excited for your day, and go to bed feeling fulfilled and grateful. Every day is a "Live-Like-You-Were-Dying" day, where you know that, no matter what happens, you have lived your life with intention and with purpose. It's a life that you look back on with awe and reverence, rather than regret.

What would you be willing to give to have a life like that? Would it be worth it to you? Whatever your dream life looks

like, I hope by now you can see that it's possible for you to
have it.

Key Points to Remember to Achieve Your Daring Life

- Remember the Be-Do-Have model? When you choose
  to be a Trailblazer, you'll do what a Trailblazer does,
  which is to take a step off the path. As you continue to
  take those steps and Clear Your Path, you will *have* a
  daring life.

- Living a daring life is the result of being a Trailblazer
  every day. It's Finding Your Bearings by questioning
  all your values and beliefs, letting go of the ones that
  aren't authentic, and living a life that is both unique to
  you and *chosen by you.*

- Living a daring life is choosing to live by your Inner
  Compass rather than your Natural Instinct. And it's
  choosing love over fear, the infinite possibility of the
  future over the limits of the past, the eternal growth of
  the soul over the temporariness of the physical. It's
  choosing yourself over the expectations of others.

Living your life in this way is nothing short of daring. To go
against the grain. To stand out and be different from the others

around you. To be vulnerable and risk being criticized, ridiculed, or rejected. While it takes courage, resilience, persistence, and strength to live this way, it is 100 percent worth it.

CHAPTER SEVENTEEN

YOU ARE A TRAILBLAZER

You've come a long way and hopefully learned some new things about yourself. You've Found Your Bearings and learned which limiting beliefs have been holding you back from the life you want. The difference between your Natural Instinct and your Inner Compass is clear to you. You know that, to get to the daring life that you want, you need to be the version of you that already has it.

One of the most important parts of being a Trailblazer is your mindset. I summarized the main points of the book into a Trailblazer Mindset to help you as you move forward and create your daring life.

Trailblazer Mindset

I Take Responsibility for My Life Adventure

I know that I am responsible for my life experience. I don't need to wait for life circumstances or other people to change. I am not a victim. If I am not happy with something in my life, I know that I have the power to change it.

I Know There Is No Perfect Guidebook

I know that no one else has the right answers for me. Those answers lie within me. There is no perfect mentor or perfect program that will solve all of my problems. Knowing this, I consume resources mindfully and with intention, using them to help me uncover the answer that lies within me.

My Value Is Unchangeable

I know that my value is fixed. I was born with it, and it's not based on my achievements or the opinions of others. I do not let others or myself question my value.

Everything Begins on the Inside

I know that anything that I am seeking must start from the inside. Rather than looking externally for the answers, I start by getting clear about my intentions, purposes, and goals, and listen for my Inner Compass before I seek outside opinions or solutions.

It's All Part of the Journey

When trials or setbacks arise, I don't worry that anything has gone wrong. I understand that life is a journey, and that it's not always supposed to be easy. Rather than focus on the negative, I choose to focus on the positive and look for the learning experiences. I don't see making mistakes as failures, but as stepping stones to my higher self.

The Only Thing That Is Certain Is That Nothing Is Certain

I don't base my decisions on certainty, because I know that nothing in life is certain. I do my research and I trust my Inner Compass to guide me to the next step. I don't let fear hold me back from doing what I know to be right. I know the what, or the bigger vision of my life, and I don't get stuck on the how. I take one step at a time and focus on moving forward.

I Make My Own Rules

I know that I don't have to do anything just because other people do it that way. I am a free thinker. I think outside of the box and am open to new ideas and ways of doing things. I allow myself to live how I want, and allow others the same. I don't need others' support, approval, or validation to do what I know is right.

Trailblazer Sisterhood

I have this vision in my mind. A woman is walking down a trail through some wild woods. She doesn't have anything but the clothes on her back. She keeps walking until the path ends at a camp. There's a tent, and a roaring fire surrounded by logs where many can gather around. This camp is surrounded by the wild, but you can see that many trails are connected to it, with the camp at the center.

The camp I'm envisioning is my camp. I've spent the last five years of my life totally dedicated to being a Trailblazer in my own life. I didn't have anyone to show me the way, and sometimes my journey felt really lonely because I didn't know many others like me. Because I don't want it to be like that for other Trailblazers, I set up this camp as a crossroads. While we all have to walk our own paths alone, I envision a community, a sisterhood of Trailblazers who come together to learn, share, and support one another on our journeys. The fact that this book ended up in your hands, and the fact that you've read it to this point, is proof that you belong to this sisterhood. I hope that, as you walk your journey, you will know that you are not alone, that many others are out there just like you, and should you ever need it, you will always have a seat around my campfire.

CONCLUSION

Remember that five-year letter the teenage me wrote in the beginning of this book? Remember how sad and disappointed I was to realize, five years later, that I hadn't fulfilled any of those dreams? In the process of writing this book, I had a realization that went unnoticed until my first draft was almost complete: every single dream that I listed in my letter has happened.

- I finished my bachelor's degree when my twins were toddlers.

- I married a man who was totally worth breaking my timeline for.

- I've had the opportunity to travel, and have been to some incredible places.

- I am now a coach who gets to help other women let go of expectations and transform their lives. I now have the career I always felt called to have.

I had completely forgotten (for the second time) about this letter and the contents within until I started writing this book. I wasn't trying to create these dreams; I hadn't even remembered them. Do you know what that tells me? It tells me that letter wasn't just a fluke. It wasn't just silly teen stuff.

—It. Was. Real.—

It was me following my Inner Compass. I didn't listen to it back then, but when I was ready, those dreams were still there, waiting for me. As I learned to follow my Inner Compass, it guided me to each and every one of those dreams.

Underneath all the expectations, limitations, obligations, and to-do lists, a part of you is waiting to be remembered. Forgotten dreams are patiently waiting for you. It's time to make those dreams a reality. Your Inner Compass will guide you to them. You're ready to follow it. You're Creating Your Path.

You are a Trailblazer.

ABOUT THE AUTHOR

Finding herself unfulfilled and unhappy, Chaundell Monn took to reading self-help books. While she was inspired by many books, she didn't find them tangible, so she forged her own path with tangible action steps. She used the Trailblazer process outlined in her book to transform her life, taking the time to do the inner work that released her from limiting beliefs and expectations. Now living an intentional life with no regrets, she works as a life coach, helping women become Trailblazers in their own lives. She wants her readers and clients to know that the path to their fulfillment and happiness is not paved by other people; the answers are all within them. When she isn't working with her clients, she loves to travel, learn new skills, spend time with her family, and read. Her mission in life is to empower women to go after their dreams and trust their Inner Compass.

COME JOIN THE TRAILBLAZER SISTERHOOD!

Even though you are walking your path alone, you don't have to feel alone. Come join me and your other Trailblazer sisters in the Trailblazer Sisterhood Facebook Group. This is a community meant to support and empower you as you continue your journey and walk your path as a Trailblazer in your own life. Come share your wins, your struggles, and make connections with other women who understand you.

www.facebook.com/groups/trailblazersisterhood

To find out how you can work with me, you can also go to my website: www.chaundellmonn.com

Made in the USA
Middletown, DE
20 December 2020